LIVING STILL, LOVING ALWAYS

ESSAYS OF A BEREAVED PARENT

NITA G. AASEN

WILSON
PUBLISHING
HOUSE

D1502717

LIVING STILL, LOVING ALWAYS
Essays of a Bereaved Parent

Copyright © 2004

Library of Congress Control Number: 2004090473

Cover design by ENVISION
St. Peter, MN

Design by Lecy Design
Minneapolis, MN

Edited by Lisa Veilleux
Manchester, NH

Printed by Printing Enterprises
New Brighton, MN

First Edition

Published by
Wilson Publishing House

For information
www.wilsonpublishinghouse.com

ISBN 0–9744317–0–2

WILSON PUBLISHING HOUSE

DEDICATION

For Erik's and David's

Father — Paul;

Brother — Kevin and sister–in–law, Pam;

Nephews — Michael and Derik;

Niece — Jenna and their

Friends Forever

ACKNOWLEDGMENTS

Living Still, Loving Always was written with the support of the following people:

Don and Lorraine Bauman, bereaved parents, who asked for permission to submit my first essay to the *National Compassionate Friends* magazine and kept on encouraging me to keep on writing. Their 17 year old son, Tom, died in a boating accident in 1975.

Judy and Rich Noyd, bereaved parents, who have been a wonderful buffer to cultural expectations on an as needed basis. Their daughter, Rene, was killed in a car accident twelve days before Erik and David. Rene and David were high school classmates.

Kathy Kurth, trusted co–worker, friend and bereaved spouse who gave me a safe place to grieve, always communicating acceptance of my new self and my grief journey. In 1997, her husband, Jerry, died at the age of 45 of complications from diabetes.

Kathy Martin, Judy Schultz, Carolyn Carlson, Carol Brown and Joanne Ardolf Decker whose permission to give voice to my grief experience came at crucial times in my ongoing grief journey.

Dr. Robert Thompson who critiqued my manuscript and provided guidance about self–publishing. His son, Paul, age 19, was killed in a car accident in 1989. Dr. Thompson's book *Remembering: The Death of a Child* was published in 2002.

Martha Potter, who also critiqued by manuscript. Her son, Patrick, age 28, was killed in an air plane crash as part of a military exercise in 1998.

Bob Albers, who generously offered to write a foreword for *Living Still, Loving Always*. Dr. Albers son, Joel, a young pastor in his first parish, was killed in a car accident in 1998. He was 28 years old at the time of his death.

Symbolizing the ongoing presence of David and Erik in their lives, the gift of a crescent moon/star pin from Bruce "Arnie" Arlt and his daughter's, Allie and Abby, provided the inspiration for the logo chosen for Wilson Publishing House.

My husband, Paul, for developing the website — **www.wilsonpublishinghouse.com**.

THANK YOU!

Erik
12/16/67–11/24/94

You were an extraordinary person.
You were born with so many wonderful gifts
and the light within you
shown so clearly for all who knew you.

Your actions were guided by courage
and an inner sense of strength;
your softly spoken words by your gentleness and truth.

My life is much richer for you chose to share these Gifts with me.
I smile when I think of you
for I remember the sparkle in your eyes,
the warmth in your heart, the Beauty in you.

YENTI A. TERRY
CLASSMATE OF ERIK
MAYO SCHOOL OF HEALTH RELATED SCIENCES

David
10/3/69–11/24/94

Is that you, Dave, that I hear?
It's been well over a year but the music of your spirit lingers on.
People still recall your smile
and they talk of you while
as they try to comprehend you're really gone.

With admiration I recall watching you walk down the hall,
greeting each student with a warm hello.
Students loved to be with you, on the courts and in class, too,
and you taught them as you helped them learn to grow.

Dave, you weren't here very long;
you had just begun your song
yet your impact isn't difficult to measure.
Talk with women, talk with men,
all say, time and again,
having known you is a gift they'll ever treasure.

DONALD HELMSTETTER
SUPERINTENDENT
BLUE EARTH AREA HIGH SCHOOL
ON THE FIRST DAY OF SCHOOL 8/96

CONTENTS

CONTENTS (Continued)

Each essay is followed by a poem or prose that captures the essay's theme. Most of these appear to be written as a tribute to the author's loved one and/or in reflection of an aspect of their grief experience. To each author whether known or unknown, thank you for giving voice to your insights born out of love and grief.

---

*Published in *We Need Not Walk Alone* and including
  A Griever's Need: A Safe Place to Come Out of the Closet (spring, 1997);
  When Words Become Gifts (fall, 2002)
  and Enduring the Unendurable (summer, 2003).
**Published in *Bereavement* and including
  Dialing Up Words of Permission: Dialing Down Words
  That Push (May/June 2003) and Finding My Voice Through Writing
  (November/December 2003).

FOREWORD

With the poignant pathos of a bereaved parent, Nita Aasen gives voice to the anguish of a *catastrophic loss* following the death of her sons. Eschewing pious platitudes and simplistic answers to inexplicable questions, she speaks with forthrightness for all of us as parents who have descended into a sea of darkness occasioned by the death of our children. Utilizing the experience of an actual tornado that devastated her hometown, she employs this image as a metaphor for the chaotic impact that this ravaging experience has on parents as they seek to deal with the unimaginable and incomprehensible nightmare associated with the death of children.

Refreshing personal candor, anecdotal stories of other grieving parents coupled with insightful research fill every page. Phrases like "no end to the never" (90) and "my feelings of emptiness were directly connected with my heaviness of heart" (128) will resonate with readers who identify with the narrative that is being shared. The persistent *shadow grief* becomes the lens through which life is viewed. The core issue as the author develops it is not to either 'get over' the grief or 'explain' the tragedy. Rather it is a perpetual effort to find some purpose of meaning for one's own life as a parent in the midst of the lingering lament. Reading this book reminds the reader that she or he is not alone in this experience. Thank you, Nita, for baring your soul and sharing your feelings, insights, and understanding.

Robert H. Albers, Ph.D.
Bereaved father

PREFACE

The lives of myself, my husband, Paul, and my surviving son, Kevin, were changed in a mere fraction of a second when my sons Erik (twenty-seven years old) and David (twenty-five years old) were killed in a freak car accident on Thanksgiving Day, 1994. While I had experienced many losses before in my life, never had I experienced anything close to what I now recognize was a "catastrophic loss."

When reading or hearing about a child's death in my pre-loss years, I would occasionally think, "I can't imagine having one (much less two) of my sons die." On those very few occasions when I tried to imagine how I might confront the death of one of my children, I quickly stopped the process. That kind of mental exercise was too disconcerting to even begin to contemplate as a possible reality.

As I discovered, there was no way I could have imagined the all-encompassing scope of such grief. The unforgiving part of this reality was that there was no escape; there was no running away from the pain. I had no other choice except to confront my grief head-on.

Early on in my grief journey, I began questioning the prevailing cultural assumption that grief resolution or healing is the eventual outcome for all losses. It became evident that our society at large does not recognize that losses vary significantly in intensity or that the impact of a catastrophic loss on one's life may result in long-term, possibly lifelong, grief.

Following the deaths of my sons, I frequently reflected on their experience with loss in their all-too-short lives. Always wanting to do their best, there were times when they did not live up to the expectations they had for themselves. Or maybe they were disappointed with a relationship or a game that was lost. But they always bounced back quickly. My perception was that their losses, on the whole, were of a lower intensity level. Perhaps they had moderate-intensity losses, but I doubt it. I am confident that they never experienced anything close to a significant or catastrophic loss.

I think of David and how he greeted his students with his signature quote: "The grass is green, the sky is blue, it's a great day to be alive." The actual weather conditions were unimportant. What was important was that he believed with every ounce of his being that life was a gift to be lived to the fullest each and every day. And he did. Now I wonder...how would David have reacted if he had experienced a catastrophic loss? If he had experienced the depths of the worst kind of emotional pain and grief?

And then I think about Erik and how he never gave up. His basketball team was 1-and-18 but they would win that next game—you bet! For an eighteen-year-old, that was optimism at its finest. (The team went 1-and-19 but their attitude and effort still made them winners.) Erik lived life intensely, drinking in each moment and savoring what life had to offer. Then he went through a period of struggling with a career decision. During that time he taped a philosophical statement on his dresser that began with the words "Life is a test."

The statements embraced by each of my sons strike a chord of truth for me. Life is a gift—a gift that is frequently taken for granted. Then a catastrophic loss shatters life to the core. For those confronting the death of a child, life is thrown completely off balance and life may be tested as never before.

In order to live with hope that life can be brought back into a semblance of balance—or stability—bereaved parents would benefit from having their "new selves" affirmed and loved. With this assurance, the hard work of readjusting their lives to fit in with their radically changed reality can begin.

TEARS

There is a time for tears.
When your heart is too full of sorrow,
they begin to flow as naturally as rain from heaven.

There is a beauty in tears, a rightness about them.
They should be shed proudly, for they show how much
you have lived and loved and lost.

Tears honor our loved ones.
There is a sacredness about them.
Each one is a prayer that only God can hear.

The soul could have no rainbows
if our eyes could have no tears.

FROM A HALLMARK CARD

TUNE IN
TO INVISIBLE NEEDS

As a nurse, I believed that my knowledge about death, loss, and grief as well as my skills in caring for terminally ill persons and supporting their family members or friends before and after their loved one's death were some of my professional strengths. That delusion was shattered the day Erik and David were killed. On that day I began my personal confrontation with the fragility of life, the excruciating pain of grief, and the emotional needs that are a consequence of such a horrific loss.

One of Erik's friends sent us a beautiful sand dollar she found while walking along an Oregon beach. I was struck not only by its beauty, but also by its fragility—how it needed to be handled with care or else it would crumble and fall apart. The fragility of that sand dollar was easy to see. Life is also fragile, but its fragility is not nearly as easy to discern. It is rather easy to take life for granted because, after all, the sun rises, the sun sets; the tide comes in, the tide goes out; the year begins, the year ends; all living things breath in and breath out; day after day, week after week, month after month, and year after year. Most of the time life seems fairly predictable, fairly stable, fairly controllable, fairly safe, and fairly comfortable. In moving through life feeling fairly confident that each of its stages and milestones will be experienced, it is rather easy to ignore the possibility that life can be incredibly fragile.

And then parents experience the death of a child or children, siblings mourn their brothers or sisters, wives or husbands lose their spouse in the young or middle adult years, sons and daughters are confronted with the death of a parent in their prime of life, or friends grieve the loss of a best friend. The fragility of life, camouflaged by a busy schedule of daily activities and the supposedly tried-and-true assumptions about life and death, becomes very obvious for those who have experienced a high-magnitude loss.

Just as the fragility of life is not readily apparent on a day-to-day basis, the variety of needs people have—physical, emotional, social, and spiritual—may or may not be visible. Case in point: On March 29, 1998, a tornado roared through our community of St. Peter, Minnesota destroying thousands of trees, breaking countless windows, tearing off roofs, leveling houses and businesses and, most tragic by far, killing a six-year-old boy. With trees clogging streets, rain pouring into houses, power and phone connections severed, and hundreds of people needing shelter, the needs of our community following that mass destruction were apparent.

The response to those needs was truly amazing. Thousands of volunteers and city and county crews from throughout the state and even from out of state came to help with the removal of downed trees and debris. Security personnel kept looters and gawkers out until personal items had been stored in a safe place. Hundreds of electricians also streamed into the community to assist with the mammoth job of restoring the power, which in some neighborhoods took longer than two weeks. In the meantime, the rather loud but comforting hum of donated generators kept many furnaces, refrigerators, and freezers going. The assistance of the Red Cross and the Salvation Army in providing food and shelter and meeting basic needs was nothing short of phenomenal. These highly visible needs had been, by and large, met!

In contrast, the emotional needs that accompany high-intensity losses are largely invisible to others. In reflecting on how needs for physical comfort or well-being are visible and therefore met, while emotional needs, being less visible, are less likely to be met, it occurred to me that an individual's emotional needs could be compared to the trees that had been in the tornado's path. Driving through town I noticed that most of the younger, smaller trees had escaped destruction, whereas the older, larger trees, being more exposed to the intensity of the tornado's power, were much more likely to have been bent, split in half, or uprooted completely.

Applying this concept to loss, it seemed reasonable to assume that one's emotional needs would reflect the intensity level of a specific loss. For instance, even though the lowest-intensity losses are the most numerous over a lifetime, only a small broken twig or two would be broken off from a small branch with each occurrence. The cumulative effect of the emotional stress following these incidents would typically be negligible. As losses increase in emotional intensity, twigs and entire branches may be broken off from one's internal trees. When the loss has a significant impact on one's life, not only are many branches broken off, but the trees may bend sharply towards the ground. At some time in life, almost everyone will likely experience a loss significant enough to bend their emotional trees. Over time, however—and it may take a long time—these trees will gradually return to an upright position, or very nearly so. These emotional trees, while bent by the loss, are not completely broken.

But the highest-magnitude loss—a catastrophic loss—can result in one's mental and emotional trees being uprooted and leveled, just as actual trees are destroyed in a tornado. And just as those who experience a natural catastrophe have no other choice but to shift their energies and efforts toward replanting trees, the bereaved also have no other choice but to begin building a new self.

Unlike the visibility associated with a natural disaster, the depth of the emotional stress following a personal tragedy is typically invisible and, consequently, unrecognized by others. In order for these invisible emotional needs to become more visible, the bereaved need to be given permission to mourn. With this strong message of acceptance, the foundation is in place to begin learning how to live with loss day by day.

In looking at the graphic portraying the loss continuum and thinking about where one's life's losses may fit on it, there is the potential for inviting comparisons such as "My loss is greater than your loss." But turning a loss experience into a sort of competitive sport would be an unfortunate misuse of the concept. When it comes to grief a me/you or we/them rivalry should be avoided at all costs. The primary purpose of the continuum is to acknowledge that losses experienced throughout a lifetime vary in intensity.

TOTAL NUMBER OF LOSSES IN LIFE

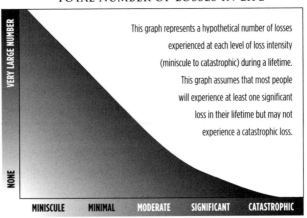

This graph represents a hypothetical number of losses experienced at each level of loss intensity (miniscule to catastrophic) during a lifetime. This graph assumes that most people will experience at least one significant loss in their lifetime but may not experience a catastrophic loss.

IMPACT OF DIFFERENT
INTENSITY LEVEL LOSSES ON LIFE

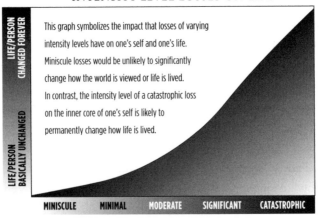

This graph symbolizes the impact that losses of varying intensity levels have on one's self and one's life. Miniscule losses would be unlikely to significantly change how the world is viewed or life is lived. In contrast, the intensity level of a catastrophic loss on the inner core of one's self is likely to permanently change how life is lived.

The impact of different levels of loss intensity is like a

Tip of twig broken from tree branch ————————————▶ Tree uprooted

PLEASE LET ME MOURN

Please let me mourn.
My child has died and I don't understand
all the emotions I am feeling.

Please let me mourn.
I may act and appear together but I am not.
Often it hurts so much I can hardly bear it.

Please let me mourn.
Don't expect too much from me.
I will try to let you know what I can and cannot handle.
Sometimes I am not always sure.

Please let me mourn.
Please don't pretend nothing has happened.
Let me talk about my child. I need to talk. It is part of grieving.
I love my child very much
and my memories are very precious to me.

Please let me mourn.
Please understand that I am not the same person
I was before my child died
and I never will be again.

Please let me mourn.
Rather than advising me how I should mourn,
please let me mourn in a way that fits for me.

Please let me mourn.
Please support me with ongoing acceptance
and love as I learn to live with grief over time
and seek to find meaning in my changed life.

ADAPTED FROM AUTHOR UNKNOWN

THOUGHTS ON CATASTROPHIC LOSS

I've thought many times since that fateful day when Erik and David were killed of all the times one gets a second chance in life— a chance to do things differently in order to have a different outcome. But in this instance, there was no second chance. There was no starting over. Instead, I found myself struggling with the expectation that the grieving process would ultimately conclude with acceptance and recovery.

The words "acceptance" and "death of a child" are clearly at odds with each other. The word "acceptance," as typically used, does not fit when one's son or daughter has died. While I have reconciled myself to the indisputable fact that my sons were killed, I cannot imagine ever saying that I accept it or agree that it is okay that it happened. It is not okay. It is not acceptable.

Another assumption that my new self vigorously questions relates to expectations for healing and recovery, regardless of the intensity of the emotional pain. Now I have grave doubts whether that premise—or promise, as some would call it—can be delivered with any certainty. While the vast majority of losses by death result in grief resolution, it is not realistic to assume that all losses, with no exceptions, will have that outcome.

What precipitates those expectations? Perhaps it is the fact that loss generally has been referred to as just that: loss. All losses— whatever kind, however intense, however life shattering—are usually lumped under the generic label of "loss" and seemingly tossed into a one-size-fits-all loss basket.

I did not think that it was quite that tidy. Consequently, when Gerald Sittser (1996) referred to expectations for recovery from a *catastrophic loss* as being unrealistic because of the far-reaching and cumulative consequences on one's self, it got my attention. Finally, I understood what made the deaths of my sons so different from all of my other losses. The grief that their deaths unleashed within my entire being—mind, body and spirit—left no doubt in my mind. I knew that I had experienced the mother of all losses: a catastrophic loss.

Learning that there was a name that described my loss could be compared to someone else finding out that her vision problem was called *glaucoma*. Being able to give my high-magnitude loss a name was a huge breakthrough that occurred about a year into my grief journey. The next step was to find out what the words *catastrophic loss* actually meant, just as someone who had been told she had glaucoma would want to know the exact meaning of that word.

In reviewing the literature there were no definitions to be found. In searching the Web the only references to catastrophic loss that popped up on the screen related to the insurance industry's description of extreme financial and property losses. That was hardly what I had in mind. The death of my sons, or any child, was about a lot more than an extreme financial loss; it was about their lives, which were cut short far before their time. No amount of money would ever bring their lives back in any way, shape, or form. Their lives were priceless.

Not finding a definition for a catastrophic loss, I decided that one was needed. So, after reading and hearing about the grief experiences of other bereaved parents, I took note of the similarities among many of us and came up with the following definition: *"A catastrophic loss is an irreversible loss that permanently changes perceptions and responses to essentially every subsequent life experience; its extremely high intensity level of emotional pain results in previously held personal beliefs, values, assumptions, and priorities being questioned, tested or shattered. The grief that is a consequence of this emotional pain is long-term and potentially lifelong.*" To put it succinctly, when a loss has changed "you" it also changes what "you" do.

Having a definition for any problem, be it physical, emotional, or mental, is often the starting point, and in many cases the turning point, in figuring out what must be done to either resolve it or manage it. Just as knowing more about the meaning of the word *glaucoma* begins to answer some of the questions about the possibility of treating it, having a definition for catastrophic loss put into words what had happened to my old self and what it would likely mean for my life.

Even though all deaths are obviously irreversible, a high-intensity loss by death is most likely to cause a radical and permanent change in how the world is viewed and life is lived. Asserting that the extremely strong love attachment parents have for their children is unparalleled in any other relationship, Kagan (Klein) (1998) logically concluded that the depth of parental love determines the depth and extent of one's emotional pain. In fact, the synergistic effect of combining these two emotions—love and pain—means that experienced together they are far more intense and painful than when there isn't a love attachment. Put another way, the death of a child is likely to activate the bomb of emotional pain like nothing else can during a lifetime.

In describing their grief, many bereaved parents used words similar to these: "There was no way I could have imagined such pervasive and encompassing emotional pain. I would never have believed I could hurt this much." In titling his book *Beyond Endurance*, Knapp (1986) captured the reactions of bereaved parents to their severe and intense grief. If that level of pain had never let up, it would truly be beyond endurance.

While I had been sad and had cried with my previous grief experiences, I had never been truly jolted or grieved for a sustained period of time. This was totally different. This was about much more than extreme sadness—about much more than frequent jags of intense crying. It was about the unrelenting ripping and repeated retching of my devastated soul seemingly trying to separate itself from the rest of me. (A rough comparison can be made to the retching that sometimes occurs after a serious bout with the flu has emptied the stomach's contents, yet the stomach, seemingly not getting the message, keeps on retching as if to eject itself from the body.) While most pain is localized to a specific area of a specific body part, this felt as if every cell was screaming. The intensity of these unyielding waves, erupting from the depth of my spirit, shattered any preconceived notion I once had about emotional pain.

Similar to the experience of other bereaved parents, I found that these raw, intense grief episodes occurred less frequently as time went on, and when they resurfaced from deep within my being, they receded more quickly. Thankfully, I have come to the point where I am usually able to control, or at least tame, the intensity of those unpredictable grief waves before they completely overpower me. And in the process, I discovered a resiliency and strength within myself that I never knew existed.

Another consequence of such a high-magnitude loss is a grief with staying power as expressed by ongoing feelings of sadness or heaviness of heart. The following nugget of bereaved wisdom acknowledging the ongoing nature of grief has been attributed to the actor Paul Newman, some years after the death of his son. "It [the grief] does not get better, it just gets different."

In coming up with the phrase *shadow grief*, Knapp may have put into words what Newman meant by "it just gets different." In hundreds of interviews, Knapp found that a majority of bereaved parents (especially mothers) continue to experience an ongoing emotional dullness or fairly constant ache and sadness regardless of the length of time it has been since their child died. He coined the phrase *shadow grief* to validate and legitimize their new normal.

Knapp saw shadow grief as being somewhat similar to a common cold in that most daily activities can be continued albeit at a somewhat diminished energy level. Even though those living with shadow grief likely function below their pre-tragedy level, the effect on most activities is not noticeable most of the time.

A breakout session at a National Compassionate Friends Conference illustrated the reality of shadow grief. The presenter began by asking two to three hundred bereaved parents how they would live their lives differently if they truly got "over it." The list they developed over the next twenty minutes eventually included the themes of regaining lost energy; not feeling as isolated, alone or lonely; alleviation of symptoms, such as a return to a pre-loss sleep pattern; and no longer thinking about their deceased children throughout the day. In other words, feeling almost "normal"—close to being their old selves again.

After pages of these items the presenter commented, "Look at all the ways you said your lives would be different if you were truly 'over it.' I looked at this list and there was one thing none of you mentioned. Can anyone tell me what that was?" Complete silence. He then said, "What none of you said was that you wouldn't be sad anymore." For many it was one of those grace-filled "aha" moments. Even if we got "over it" (according to the list) the sadness, the lingering pain (our never-ending common cold) would still be there.

There was solace in knowing that I was not alone in having sadness as a shadow in my life. Also, rather than being confronted with lofty expectations for healing and recovery, it seemed much more reasonable to think about learning how to live with sadness. With that shift in thinking, I had some hope that I could and would endure if I made a concerted effort each and every day.

I have been asked if it is possible to mourn without becoming a long-term griever. The short answer: It happens all the time. With all my other personal losses, my grief had been resolved without any significant changes in how I perceived myself or my world. I came through all those losses with my old self intact and had never considered referring to myself as "bereaved."

As I began reading about parental grief I found that the phrase *bereaved parent* put into words the incredibly high cost parents have paid when their child's death thrusts them into a group they could have never imagined joining and from which there is no escape clause and no expiration date. While I still have three sons, only one is still living. As a result, being a bereaved mom has become part of my identity.

So how did this identity change impact my life? While I may have outwardly appeared to look the same to those who had not spent any extended time with me, I was aware that shadow grief had toned down my energy level as my step had lost some of its bounce or buoyancy. Besides having eyes that felt strained, my voice inflections also had fewer ups and downs. When it came to non-grief-related issues, former big deals were no longer big deals. Strangely, I felt calmer; it took something really important to get a rise out of me.

I have, in fact, been told that I look serene and/or calm. Initially that took me by surprise, but then I remembered reading this analogy in a Compassionate Friends Newsletter:

> Bereaved parents are like a duck
>
> **Above the surface** looking composed and unruffled
>
> **Below the surface** paddling like crazy!

So it may not have been so unusual, after all, that in responding with less energy or gusto to life experiences, I may have appeared serene. Just below the surface, however, I was treading hard, struggling to keep my head above water so I could "go on" to find a way to learn how to live with loss.

Living with loss could be thought of as being similar to living with any other disability or chronic condition that changes how a person functions each and every day. There are no time-outs or vacations from a speech deficit, arthritis, or any disability for that matter. Instead, when these life-changing events occur, the ability to function is limited in one way or another. And so it is with a catastrophic loss. In changing how bereaved parents feel, think, and perceive their inner and outer worlds, it inevitably changes how many of them function in their daily lives.

So what makes it possible to learn how to live with sadness? C.S. Lewis, (1961) commented that "Sorrow needs not a map, but a history." When bereaved parents are given permission and encouragement to grieve in their own way, they can grieve at their own pace without an hourglass dangling in front of them. With unique circumstances surrounding the death event, the deceased, and the griever, there is no reliable road map showing the way. The bereaved must build his or her own road.

Even though the path will likely be filled with potholes and detours, the most reliable compass for the bereaved to take on their grief journey is likely to reside in the depths of their inner selves— a trust in their own intuition and a belief in their own inner strengths and resources. Then, with appropriate support, more energy and effort can be directed towards accommodating the death of a child into one's life over time.

THERE IS NO WORD

They call a man a widower
when he has lost his wife.

The woman is a widow
when her man does lose his life.

And orphan is the word perhaps
for most of us one day.

For it's normal losing
Mom and Dad along the way.

But you can look both high and low
and then look far and wide

And never find a word for one
Who's had a child who died.

So, how is it that even in a
lectionary

And, like some unfound jungle plan,
There's yet no name for me?

Or could it be a word that's just
too difficult to choose?

And God forbid; a nightmare curse,
too horrible to use?

So, at a loss to tell our loss,
we call ourselves bereaved.

For there's no word to tell of pain
that cannot be believed.

KEN FALK, TCF OF NORTHWESTERN CT
TCF NEWSLETTER FAIRMONT CHAPTER, 01/99

THE BLESSINGS
OF SHOCK

When I think back to the earliest days of my grief journey, I remember being amazed that I kept on functioning, at least most of the time. I went through the public rituals—visitation, funeral, and reception—choking up at times, but otherwise responding appropriately, accepting condolences, even comforting others, and, strangely, scarcely shedding any tears. And I thought, "How come I'm not falling apart?" I was also able to make decisions regarding the funeral, giving directions and suggestions about what to include in the service. Later I wondered, "When my world had been so totally destroyed, how did I keep myself together so I could think about all those details?" In a sense, it felt as if *shock had detached my thinking, feeling self from my physical self so that I could continue to function, somewhat like a robot, while the rest of me was protected from grasping the reality of the tragedy.* I have come to think of it as a kind of surreal "out-of-body" experience. The blessing of shock.

Subsequently, I have gone to visitations and funerals at which other bereaved parents have appeared so "together." Again, I marveled at how shock helped them go through the unfathomable motions of planning a memorial service for their son or daughter. It was only because I had been there, done that, that I realized what made it possible for a bereaved parent to appear to be so on top of it. *When there is no other choice, shock made it possible to do the impossible.* The blessing of shock.

One of the initial responses of many bereaved parents, immediately following the death of their child, is to make some type of philosophical or religious statement. For example, within the hour of my sons' deaths I made the totally true comment "Erik and David were such gifts. We were so blessed to have them as part of our lives for as long as we did" and remained composed and in control. I appeared to be taking my personal catastrophe in stride. Observing other bereaved parents responding in a like manner, the nonbereaved may erroneously conclude that anyone who can handle a tragedy with such grace under fire must be inordinately strong and courageous. Much later I realized that these philosophical or belief statements, while genuinely sincere at the time, are typical of mourners who have been jettisoned into extreme shock. In such cases, *shock becomes the primary force behind the facade of courage and strength.* The blessing of shock.

But, at other times, I was immobilized. I would be sitting on the sofa, vaguely hearing the bustle in the kitchen, and I didn't lift a finger to help. I just sat there—shell-shocked. Normally, I would have been incensed if anyone had come into my kitchen without my explicit permission and taken charge of organizing the meals. But then I thought with gratitude, "What would I have done if someone had not been there to take over and do what needed to be done?" *Shock let me let others do what I could not do for myself.* The blessing of shock.

During those first few days the presence of my sons' friends filled the house. They came or called from all over the country to support us and each other. They shared stories I had never heard—poignant stories, memories of good times and challenging times. They were also very clear in stating that death would not end their friendship; Erik and David would be their "friends forever." As a tribute to David, some of these friends put together a video showing him in his element, teaching tennis and hamming it up. *And unbelievably, right in the midst of our profound grief, we found ourselves laughing, spontaneously and genuinely.* Definitely, the blessing of shock.

Shock, however, has its limits. On the first night following the accident, the stress and grief became so great it broke through the shock defense and I began shaking and screaming. In other words, I lost it. As I began to feel just the tiniest bit of the total horror and pain of a parent's worst nightmare doubled, I was given an introduction to what lay ahead of me grief-wise. The doctor was called. I was given a mild sedative and shock resumed control again. Over time, shock withdrew its numbing benefits and I began experiencing episodes of deep emotional pain that had been beyond my wildest imagination. *By experiencing the pain in shorter spurts, intense as they were, I continued to be protected from feeling the totality of the pain.* The blessing of shock.

In being nature's cushion against the unbearable, *the multiple blessings of shock were a vital protection during the initial months and beyond. With that realization came the hope that whatever came after shock wore off could be endured and survived.*

Grief tears us apart
with the reckless abandon
of a tornado.

HAIKU BY DIANTHA AIN
BEREAVEMENT MAGAZINE
JULY/AUGUST 2003

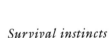

Survival instincts
spontaneously kick in
when tragedy strikes.

HAIKU BY DIANTHA AIN
BEREAVEMENT MAGAZINE
MAY/JUNE 2001

ABUNDANT HUGGING:
A SOURCE OF SOLACE

Immediately after Erik and David's friends and our friends and coworkers learned about the accident, they were either calling us by phone or dropping everything to come to our home. The outpouring of support from our community and the communities in which our sons had lived was overwhelming. We were surrounded by love and concern. Among the deluge of visitors, flowers, memorials, and cards was one card with just three words written on it: "Words are inappropriate." I remember thinking, "He's got that right." In being right, those words were, in fact, very appropriate. A paradox, to be sure!

In those first numbing weeks and months, I heard many wonderful stories and reflections about Erik and David. Beyond that, I remember very little of what was said. But what I remember and treasure was the constant presence of people and the HUGS. Prior to the accident, and true to my Swedish-American roots,* I had been an extremely cautious and selective hugger. Not any more! Grief transformed me into what might be called a rather "promiscuous" hugger. In fact, I attribute much of my being able to survive those

---

*For those unfamiliar with Swedish/Scandinavian traits, we tend to be reluctant to show outward expressions of affection and are rather stingy with our praise. For example, after attending a superb concert, most people would rave enthusiastically, "Wasn't that a super concert!!" whereas the Swedish American might grudgingly admit with only a slight change in voice inflection, "Oh yeah, I guess it was pretty good." (Translation: It was a top-of-the-line performance). In picking up this phrase from me, David would smile broadly and say, "Pretty good, huh, Mom?" when he thought something was excellent. But there was nothing stingy about his hugging—David was a master hugger, despite his Scandinavian heritage.

first weeks to being hugged and held—over and over again. They were hugs of solace from people I knew well and from my sons' friends, many of whom I knew, but many of whom I met only after the accident. It made no difference. It seemed so natural to reach out to hug and be hugged.

I had never experienced such abundant and spontaneous hugging before. Wrapping me up firmly and securely in their arms was a tangible way that others could help me bear this indescribable pain. These were no ordinary hugs—they were extraordinary—master hugs, cream-of-the-crop hugs.

Studies have shown that in order to thrive, every person should be touched or hugged each day. Through its countless nerve endings, the skin—typically hungry to be touched, hungry to be hugged— becomes hungrier after loss. After Erik's and David's deaths—when the emotional pain was so raw, so acute—my skin seemed to be starving. I craved the solace that came from being touched and hugged.

And, then, there were the eyes filled with tears of disbelief and pain beyond belief. To paraphrase a song written by professional folk singers and friends of David, the eyes said, "Friend of mine, I will stand with you. As you begin to bear this load, you do not need to walk this road alone." Solace was given through the eyes—eyes that spoke louder than actual words.

But being human, the tendency is to want to say *something*. But what words can be said when words are inappropriate? Because they fear that their child will be forgotten, many bereaved parents say time and again that the two words that ease those fears is hearing their son or daughter's name spoken out loud. To illustrate, years after the accident, my husband and I were at David's college alma mater for a holiday event. As I was in the dessert line, a lady came up to me and said, "I saw your name tag. By any chance, are you *David Aasen's* mom?" After doing a double take (it had been some time since I had been asked what used to be a rather common question), I said with much surprise and appreciation, *"Yes, I am!"* With those two unexpected words, this person gave me five memorable gifts.

Her first gift was saying David's name out loud. She didn't just think to herself, "Hmmm, I bet that's David Aasen's mom, but I better not say anything." *She said something.* Then, acknowledging that I'm still a mom was an all-important second gift. While my sons' deaths had resulted in my becoming a bereaved mother, death could not take away the fact that I am, and always will be, Erik and David's mom. The third gift came about when she told me how her daughter, a classmate of David's, continued to treasure the friendship they had shared.

Giving me permission to share a bit of my grief journey was her fourth gift. I told her that there hadn't been any truly easy, carefree, feeling-on-top-of-the-world days since my sons' deaths and how taking each day as it came had become the most doable way for me to go on. Her fifth gift was the manner in which she asked her questions. In feeling valued for being honest, I didn't feel obligated to cover up my grief, and my integrity remained intact. The warmth of those gifts has lingered on in my heart and has comforted me.

But words or phrases meant to be supportive may turn out to have the opposite effect. A bereaved friend related how the words "comforting memories" came up in conversations. While many of her memories were indeed comforting, there were others that tended to be disturbing, unsettling, and haunting, especially when sleep was hard to come by. In other words, memories also have the power of hitting the bereaved with the full force of all that has been lost. Additionally, many sympathy cards infer that memories are the magical antidote to grief. While many memories are treasured, the assumption that they will somehow neutralize or lessen a person's sadness or help fill the huge, gaping chasm in his or her life does not take into account the intensity of a catastrophic loss experience.

The nuances and ambiguities of words describing grief may be perceived differently following a child's death, and communicating about sorrow with the nonbereaved may become more difficult. Words are, by their very nature, limited and flawed. There simply are no words that could even begin to capture the feelings of bereaved parents following the death of their son or daughter. Words are, indeed, inappropriate.

Consequently, it is not surprising to find that in the first days, weeks, and months following a child's death, there is remarkable consistency in what bereaved parents find to be most comforting. The words that are said are generally not nearly as important as being surrounded by the presence of loved ones, looking into eyes that talk and hugging—hugging abundantly!

HUGS

No moving parts, no batteries
No monthly payments and no fees
Inflation proof, non-taxable
In fact, it's quite relaxable.

It can't be stolen, won't pollute
One size fits all, do not dilute
The energy it takes is minimal
But its results are continual.

Your circulation it corrects
Without unpleasant side effects
It's the best of all prescriptions
For easing any buildup of tensions.

What fits this description?
What is it that helps us function?
What is it that feels so cozy and snug?
What else except a comforting and loving HUG!

Adapted from Author Unknown

SHATTERED TO THE CORE I:
IMPACT ON ASSUMPTIONS, BELIEFS, VALUES

On that horrific day when Erik and David were killed, my life was shattered in an instant. A consequence of this shake-up was that the assumptions, beliefs, values, and priorities that had provided the solid ground for making decisions about my life were blown apart, forcing me to question and test these guiding principles for their continued relevance and meaning in my life.

To get an idea of what happened when I was forced to confront the ongoing applicability of these principles for my life, visualize the effects of a sudden force striking glass. At the instant a glass item is smashed, pieces and fragments of all sizes and shapes scatter in all directions. Some may become embedded in the ground, never to be found. The countless shards of glass and lost pieces dash any hope that all the holes and cracks can be repaired. Even if all the pieces *could* be glued together, the cracks and chips would be a constant reminder that the glass had been broken and would never be the same again.

Likewise, the deaths of my sons created huge, gaping holes in my old self that made restoration impossible. The inner core of my old self was essentially destroyed, leaving only a gutted shell of devastated emptiness. Many bereaved parents use strikingly similar words to describe the impact of their children's deaths on their lives. From a bereaved mother: "I told others that I was amazed that the death of my [only] two children didn't kill me. Now [months later] I realize it had, in fact, killed me...and a new me would need to emerge from the ashes." From a bereaved father: "My interior life was destroyed like the havoc and chaos occasioned by a violent windstorm." To symbolize how one's old self has been shattered, I have thought—somewhat facetiously and somewhat seriously—that there would be some merit in having some kind of ritual acknowledging that reality.

As the tremors radiated out from the depths of my inner self, the ground shifted and moved about, making it difficult to regain a sense of balance. But that was the task set before me. In order to achieve a sense of stability I needed to figure out which of my assumptions, beliefs, values, and priorities continued to fit, which ones needed to be revised, and which ones would be sent to the trash bin because of their irrelevance in my new life.

Assumptions: Prior to the deaths of my sons, my experience with tragedy had been limited to hearing or reading about the disasters of others. Even though I was well aware that catastrophes happen every day, they had always been someone else's bad luck. In reading or talking about these events, I would think rather casually, "There but for the grace of God go I." Actually, I took it as a matter of fact that by the grace of God, my sons would keep on progressing from one milestone to another without any major interruptions.

I had the basic assumption that my sons would outlive me. I took it for granted that until the time of my death, I would see them work, play, relax, talk, laugh, worry, care, love, play with their nephews and niece, and one day become proud fathers and do all those "Dad" kinds of things. While I didn't have any set expectations regarding the frequency of phone calls or personal visits, the one huge expectation I had was that they would stay alive. Ab–so–lute–ly!

I had also assumed that by praying—for a safe journey, good health, or whatever—God would listen to and comply with my reasonable requests. I had assumed that if I planned for the future, tomorrow would come; I could count on it. In all honesty, I had the illusion that I could control my family's health and safety—that no matter where my sons were or what they were doing, through sheer willpower and love I could somehow protect them from danger. Rosof (1994) refers to these illusions as being symbolic of an invisible canopy of love and protection that parents erect and place over their children to keep them safe.

Instead I learned that control is limited; actions taken to safeguard one's family from tragedy may influence the outcome in some situations, but there are never any guarantees. None! Zero! My sons' lives were snuffed out in an instant. At that moment, the canopy of love and protection was shredded and any illusions I had about the stability of life were shattered. Death knows no boundaries. There are no class distinctions. Everyone is equal. Anyone, at any place or any time, can just be one short breath away from death. Life is incredibly fragile!

Beliefs: When the 200-mile-per-hour tornado train zipped through our community, more than 20,000 trees were destroyed. The vast majority of trees destroyed were older and larger, leaving the younger, more supple and flexible trees to carry on. And isn't that how life is supposed to be? The expectation is that the generation in the winter of their years will die before those in an earlier season of life. But then my sons died, defying the natural order by dying out of order. The cries of "Where's the justice?" "Where's the fairness?" endlessly echoed and rebounded off each other. And the cries continued, "They were just beginning to come into their own! They were in the prime of life. They had so much to live for, so much to offer."

"Why God, why my sons? Why our family? What did we do to deserve this?" But then I also needed to ask, "Why not us?" Why should my family be spared from tragedy any more than any other family? Why should we be given preferential treatment? That wouldn't be fair. But then, life isn't fair!

Do tragedies happen because prayers were not convincing enough, not genuine enough, not long enough, not often enough? Is it because beliefs were not strong enough, not powerful enough, or not forceful enough? To be sure, the rain falls on the just and unjust alike, but that doesn't quiet the questions, the incessant *whys* of such a tragedy.

It's clear that fervent prayers for a safe journey, for example, often fall short with statistics showing that for every x number of miles traveled, x number of people will be killed. On Thanksgiving Day, 1994, that x number included my two sons along with others. The statistics that I had once read about in the newspaper with a sense of detachment now included my children. It was no longer another faceless story. I could no longer just turn the page and put it out of my mind; I was living the headlines.

Having my world blown apart posed the ultimate challenge to my belief system. The beliefs that I had accepted as gospel, so to speak, since childhood were seriously questioned and tested for the first time. I felt that I had been deserted and abandoned by God. The words of a song, "Have I lost God or has he lost me?" captured my anguish and uncertainty regarding my beliefs about life and death and, more to the point, life after death.

In questioning these beliefs, many bereaved parents are confronted with tried-and-true one-liners such as "Your children are safe with God." While these answers are meant to be the spiritual medicine that will take the pain away, they usually fall far short of the mark. For me, the primary issue with these platitudes was that they discouraged me from continuing to openly explore and examine my doubts and hard questions head-on with others. Instead of giving me permission to work through my struggles about my beliefs and encouraging an open, honest discussion having a wide range of perspectives, these answers typically shut down conversations.

I was not necessarily looking for answers to my "why" questions. I knew that there were no "for sure" answers to the ultimate mysteries about life and death. Instead, what I needed was the recognition and acknowledgment that these questions were legitimate; that I had a right to ask and ponder these questions; that they were normal questions to ask following a child's death. While searching for these answers was similar to looking for the proverbial needle in a haystack, having permission to ask the hard questions freely would have encouraged me to live the questions. Without that gift, answers became more elusive.

In working through a challenge to their belief system, some bereaved parents end up with beliefs very similar to those of their "old self" while others adjust or revise their beliefs in minor to major ways. Still others construct an entirely new set of beliefs for their "new self."

Value/Priority Changes: Ann Finkbeiner (1996) uses the concept of a "zero point" to describe the dramatic change that occurs in the values and priorities of bereaved parents. The zero point, on a hypothetical scale, defines the point that separates values or priorities of significant importance from those of less importance. Priorities and values on the plus side of the zero point have a high priority whereas those listed on the minus side of the zero point have a low priority. Prior to the death of a child there may have been many things on the plus side of the zero point that reflected one's priorities or values, such as sports, social status, career advancement, the drive to be "number one," being a consummate consumer, or accumulating wealth.

Following a catastrophic loss, the scale is typically reset at zero with *everything starting over* because *everything looks different.* Priorities or values that had been on the plus side of the zero point shift instantaneously to the minus side. All the symbols of success and the trappings of the world suddenly become irrelevant. After interviewing parents who have been bereaved for up to twenty-five years, Finkbeiner concludes that the only values remaining on the plus side of the zero point following a child's death are those directly connected to love, life, and death. All other values, which had been perceived as being indispensable for living the good life, are either deleted completely or plummet to the low end of the priority scale.

Reflecting on his changed values and priorities, Nicholas Wolterstorff (1987) stated, "My attachment to the world is loosened...I can do without them…What the world gives I still accept, but what it promises, I no longer reach for." Likewise, my attachment to material items and places has markedly lessened. In needing the things of the world only for their functional purpose—the exception being memory-related items and family heirlooms—my values about what is truly important or necessary have changed significantly.

When a catastrophic loss has resulted in a major overhaul of one's guiding principles for life, it inevitably changes how life is viewed or perceived. Like many other bereaved parents, I find myself referring to many life experiences as happening either before or after my sons' deaths. Drawing this line in the sand, so to speak, marks the precise moment my life changed forever. It matters not if it is a significant or insignificant event—it is perceived differently post-loss than it would have been pre-loss. Activities connected with all of the seasons—such as walking through the snow in winter, smelling apple blossoms in spring, watching a sunset in the summer, or hearing a flock of geese fly by in the fall—have different feelings and thoughts attached to them.

LIFE WAS PERFECT

In the days when life was fine
And the sun shone bright,
We laughed and planned and dreamed.
We danced in the warmth of love.

We believed that life was perfect.

Our children learned to walk and talk,
We nursed them through childhood illnesses.
And worried when they learned to drive.
We grew together, nurtured with love.

We believed that life was perfect.

Then, our eldest daughter became ill.
We didn't realize what the diagnosis
would come to mean.
Nothing very bad could happen to us.

We believed that life was perfect.

Sometimes, love and hope and medicine
Do not make an illness disappear.
Sometimes, the unimaginable happens,
And we are left wondering what happened to

The life that was perfect.

The loss of a child of any age
Is devastating to the entire family.
We were unable to help our child.
We look back and remember when,

We believed that life was perfect.

JUDITH FRIEDMAN
BEREAVEMENT MAGAZINE
JANUARY/FEBRUARY, 2003

SHATTERED TO THE CORE II:
IMPACT ON PERCEPTIONS

Life experiences change perceptions. Prior to the tornado, for instance, I would have given a storm having winds of 100-miles-per-hour a ranking of eight or nine on a ten-point scale. Once I experienced the wrath of a tornado having winds of 200-miles-per-hour, I understood that it was completely different from any other storm I had encountered or would likely encounter again in my lifetime. Suddenly, winds of 100-miles-per-hour were given a lower ranking of five or six, whereas the tornado was rated a ten on the scale. No doubt about it. My perceptions had changed.

Just as a 200-mile-per-hour tornado is an uncommon occurrence, a catastrophic loss of an extremely high intensity level is equally uncommon and well outside of normal limits. Reflecting on his loss experiences prior to his child's death, a grief-stricken dad had given his most intense losses an eight or nine on a scale of ten. When that score was propelled off the scale by the staggering pain brought about by his son's death, those events were seen from a completely different perspective and given a score of two.

Some of the most far-reaching and profound perception changes following the death of a child are frequently associated with emotional responses, relationship shifts, and feelings about death and dying.

Emotional Responses: Media messages routinely project the image that happiness and having fun are an inherent component of the American way of life. These standards represent a steep emotional mountain for many grievers. Wolterstorff (1987) put it this way: "Perhaps what is over is happiness as the fundamental tone of my existence—now sorrow is that. Sorrow is no longer the islands but the sea." And so it has been!

A common assumption holds that ongoing sadness is a bona fide symptom of clinical depression. Believing that the term "deep sadness" more accurately describes parental grief than "depression," Kagan (Klein) (1998) rejects that assumption and backs it up with two major ways these terms differ for bereaved parents. First, bereaved parents have no difficulty naming the reason for their deep sadness, whereas the cause of other types of nonclinical depression cannot always be identified. Second, deep sadness likely has no defined end point, whereas most instances of nonclinical depression are likely resolved, either with or without treatment.

Further clarifying the difference between the sadness of grief and sadness of depression, Schneider (1994) recognizes that bereaved parents focus their attention not on themselves, as is the case with clinical depression, but on the death of their child and his or her lost future. More hopefully, an additional difference is that those living with deep sadness continue to respond to touch, warmth, and reassurance and actively search for a reason to keep on living, whereas those experiencing clinical depression are more likely to feel like giving up on life. Reading about deep sadness provided me with one of those "that's it" moments. It described me to a T.

Living with deep sadness has had a major impact on my emotional responses to life experiences. The natural emotional highs that had normally ebbed and flowed through life have been essentially lopped off. Perhaps one way this change could be represented would be to symbolically toss all the letters in the positive feeling words up in the air. When they landed, "enjoy" might be spelled "jnyoe" or "fun" would become "unf" to convey that pre-loss feelings, while still present, have been toned down or muted by sadness post-loss. Another statement, which referred to "work and play becoming more focused and serious" for bereaved parents, also resonated with my new self

(Bernstein, 1997). My increased respect for the fragility and brevity of life has resulted in a serious search for a mission that would bring a sense of focus and purpose to each day.

Perceptions about what is regarded as humorous are also likely to change as a result of parental grief. To illustrate, in sharing an experience with a group of bereaved parents, I said, "The other day I woke up feeling sadder than my normal sad." I was startled when laughter immediately filled the room. For a brief second, I wondered what was so funny. Just as quickly, I realized they were laughing because those words also reflected their reality—their "new normal." No explaining was necessary. They knew exactly what I meant because it had been their experience as well. For a few wonderful moments I wrapped myself up in the comforting and welcome sound of their support. Afterwards I thought how puzzling that statement and laughter would have seemed to the nonbereaved. In like manner, bereaved parents frequently find that situations or comments that had been perceived as funny before their child died are no longer as humorous.

Another emotional change related to my not becoming scared as easily. Using another tornado analogy, pre-loss I would have been terrified of being home alone as the tornado bore down on our neighborhood. I would have feared for my life and my house. Instead, as the debris went flying by, I calmly observed, "So this is what a tornado is like." I felt no heart-pounding fear. As I climbed the basement steps and opened the door to find an intact house, I also felt no real relief. I was well aware that any loss of personal property would have seemed minor and inconsequential compared to Erik's and David's deaths.

Continuing his reflections about how his perceptions about life had changed following his son's death, Wolterstorff's words provided another powerful image of how grief continued to shadow his life. "The zest is gone, the passion is cooled, the striving quieted...instead of rowing, I float." My new self resonated with each of those statements. The balloon of life had sprung a leak and descended to a lower level. Before my sons' deaths there was a lot of gusto available to propel me through the days; now I just kind of lollygag along. Consequently, trying to put a cap on the leak in the balloon of life in order to "go on" even though the zest is gone has become a major focus of my energies and efforts.

Relationship Shifts: Following the death of a child, the overriding change is that relationships that had been balanced have suddenly become imbalanced.

The immediate change that occurred at the instant of my sons' deaths was that the vast majority of future references about them would, of brutal necessity, be in the past tense. Without a present or future, time had stopped, and any mention of their names would be limited to what *was* instead of what *is* or *will be*. Being totally unaware of the implications of this reality, nonbereaved friends and family members innocently chattered on about their children's comings and goings, not recognizing how painful it was to me to never again be able to chatter on about my children. The invisible gap between their lives as they were being described and my life as I was experiencing it was huge.

Typically, many friendships form and continue because of shared interests such as political campaigns, church meetings, community projects, music events, or any number of activities. If activities such as attending school events are the primary reason for the relationship, the death of a child severs this connecting link, and there may be nothing else to replace it. More telling, when the dramatic shift in perceptions and priorities is not matched by a similar shift in one's family and friends view of life, the mutual needs and expectations for the relationship will likely change as well.

Another feeling that typically rises to the surface is the feeling of aloneness when there is no one in a bereaved parent's family or social circle who truly understands what it means to be a bereaved parent.

Even though they hope that all parents could be spared from knowing the depth, breadth, and scope of this pain, not being able to talk to someone who has walked a similar walk may leave them feeling very alone.

As a consequence of this feeling of aloneness, bereaved parents may feel disconnected from the typical social bantering and chitchat that is typically part of "passing the time of day." To use some current jargon, this feeling of isolation resulted in my internal mute button being clicked on. Instead of feeling actively engaged or connected with events, I observed and reacted as if from a distance to the goings-on around me. In short, my revised assumptions, beliefs, values, and priorities had resulted in my new self struggling to fit in with what had once been "ordinary" conversations for my old self.

According to Riches and Dawson (1996), the boundary separating the world of bereaved parents from the nonbereaved is extremely wide. Being unable to fathom the changed emotional landscape of those experiencing a child's death, caring others vastly underestimate the devastating impact of that event. Without an understanding of the totality of the change that has occurred within the inner selves of bereaved parents, the nonbereaved are unintentionally oblivious to the effort and energy it takes for grievers to get the gears of their lives moving again after it has come to a screeching halt. They are genuinely unaware of the immense disconnect or gap between the two worlds.

A final caveat: Bereaved parents have said time and time again that they continue to have a relationship with their deceased child; that their son or daughter is still an essential part of their "present" lives. In contrast, for others the death is perceived as ending the relationship; the relationship became part of their past, a part of their history.

With such varying perspectives about the "present" between bereaved parents and their nonbereaved friends, restoring the balance or finding enough common ground to maintain the relationship may become more difficult. And if it had been assumed that the relationship would eventually return to the "way it was," the disappointment and sense of loss that accompanies the realization that there can be no going back may catch everyone involved off guard. Ultimately, if pre-loss friendships or activities no longer mesh with their new selves, many bereaved parents find that there are either fewer names or different names in their address book.

Fear of Death: Another reality encountered in life is the mortal nature of the human condition. A common response to that indisputable fact is to think and talk about death as infrequently and superficially as possible. In contrast, thoughts about life, death, and life after death tend to increase markedly for bereaved parents.

In fact, death may no longer be perceived as the worst thing that could happen. In changing the phrase "sentenced to death" to "sentenced to life," another bereaved parent captured how the death of his son completely reversed his perception about death and dying. Darcie Sims, a well-known presenter at Compassionate Friends conferences, stated that the hardest part of her grief journey was coming to terms with the fact that her son had died and she had not.

Because many parents would have willingly traded places with their child and died instead of them, another major shift in their thinking is that they tend to fear death less. This perception shift appears to be solidly linked to the hope that death will reunite them with their son or daughter. In exploring the concept of life after death, Knapp (1986) found that a commonality among bereaved parents is their belief that their child lives on in some kind of spirit or energy form. This is also true for most parents who did not have this conviction prior to the death of their child. It is simply unacceptable to consider the possibility that one's child could be totally obliterated, having no substance, following the death event.

In anticipating this reunion, I find myself wondering, "What will Erik and David look like? Will they be there to meet me and recognize me at the moment of my death?"

Since the form our spirit takes on after death continues to be a mystery, I had not been able to visualize what my reunion with my sons might be like until I read the book, "Fireflies" (1988) written by David Morrell. Following the death of his son, Matthew, Morrell had a vision of a place where there were an infinite number of wondrous fireflies zooming and spinning around. Instinctively he felt that these brilliantly colored fireflies were rapturous souls. His eyes quickly fixated on one specific firefly which he intuitively knew was his son. Fast-forwarding to the moment of his own death, Morrell imagined one very special firefly breaking away from the zooming and spinning multitude to welcome him.

Indeed, if one continues to exist as a spirit after death, then I have imagined that there will be two fireflies greeting me with those wonderful, but soundless, words that I have not heard for so long: "Hi, Mom!" Then, flashing their incredible (spirit) smiles, they will gather me up in their strong (spirit) arms and hold me tight. With this vision of ultimately being reunited with my sons, my fear of death has been largely removed.

The ripple effect of my changed or revised assumptions, beliefs, and values on my perceptions was ultimately reflected in the very depths of my being. Similar to other bereaved parents, this has involved much more than some minor tinkering around the edges. It has involved a major rebuilding, and I have become a very different person.

RISE UP SLOWLY, ANGEL

Rise up slowly, Angel.
I cannot let you go.
Just drift softly midst the faces,
In sorrow now bent low.

Ease the searing anger,
Born in harsh, unyielding truth
That Death could steal my loved one
From the glowing blush of youth.

Rise up slowly, Angel.
Do not leave me here, alone,
Where the warmth of mortal essence
Lies replaced by cold hard stone.

Speak to me in breezes,
Whispered through the drying leaves,
And caress my brow with raindrops
Filtered by the sheltering trees.

Rise up slowly, Angel.
For I cannot hear the song
Which calls you through the shadows
Into the light beyond.

Wrap me in a downy cape
Of sunshine, warm with love,
And kiss a tear-stained mother's face
With moonlight from above.

Then, wait for me at sunset,
Beside the lily pond,
And guide me safely homeward
To your world, which lies beyond.

Just spread your arms to take me
In reunion's sweet embrace,
And we shall soar together,
To a different time and place.

DIANE ROBERTSON, BEREAVEMENT MAGAZINE
NOVEMBER/DECEMBER 2001

SHATTERED TO THE CORE III:
IMPACT ON THE REST
OF YOUR LIFE

One bereaved parent visualized a catastrophic loss as being somewhat like an octopus, which used its tentacles to penetrate and reach into every nook and cranny of her life. The impact of this event on the lives of many bereaved parents might also be compared to a game of dominoes in which every domino that had provided some sense of stability and predictability in life falls down. It marks the instant when their lives changed and, in all likelihood, becomes the defining point of their lives.

In contrast, parents whose children have not died likely refer to a milestone in their life, such as the birth of a child, marriage, or some accomplishment, as their primary defining point. From my vantage point, the primary difference between the defining points of a milestone or happy event and an extremely high-intensity loss experience is the impact those occasions have on one's inner self. Milestones or happy occasions affirm or strengthen the foundation of one's core self. In contrast, those same assumptions, beliefs, values, and priorities are shattered following a child's death. The difference is huge and the impact it has had on my life is also huge.

A major shift in my thinking related to how I looked at the future. My old self was always looking ahead—anticipating the next house project, the next tennis match, the next vacation, the next this or the next that. And the sky was usually clear and mostly sunny; for as far as I could see there were no big storms on the horizon of my tomorrows. Now my new self, being mindful that there may be no tomorrow, lives life much more in the present—one day at a time.

What used to get me all bent out of shape no longer fazes me. By not sweating the small stuff, it is much easier to take life experiences such as traffic jams, water in the basement, rabbits in the garden, loss of credit cards, outcome of a political issue, or not winning the big game in stride. These events have ceased to elicit a charged emotional response, positive or negative. But, conversely, my patience and tolerance for gossiping, petty complaining, and bickering about trivial matters that ultimately are of little consequence are at a much lower level. In short, I have gotten rid of much of the clutter that took up much of my pre-loss life.

Many bereaved parents also tend to view personal obligations differently. When motivations change, job or volunteer activities may take on a different focus. Some relate that having a routine gives them the push that is needed to get up and get going in the morning. For others, having a schedule of tasks that need to be completed provides a structure that gets them through the day. In order to keep on functioning, many welcome the distraction of becoming involved in volunteer work. Still others need to scale back on what they had typically been involved in prior to their child's death. Participation in leisure-related activities or hobbies may be at either a markedly lowered or increased energy level.

With a changed worldview, the trees do not block the view of the forest quite as easily or quite as naively. Similar to many bereaved parents, I've placed a higher value on finding solutions to moral and social issues that will result in permanent, long-term effects rather than on temporary, short-term fixes. In many situations, answers to complex problems have become grayer, less black and white, making it easier to withhold judgment and consider varying perspectives. In contrast, issues connected with the prevention of accidental or untimely deaths have become more clearly defined as right or wrong.

Without as much to lose anymore, and especially if the issue has resulted or could result in a child's death, it may become easier for bereaved parents to risk challenging the status quo and speak out on such controversial social problems as gun control or youth access to alcohol. Many experiencing parental grief also give themselves permission to live on the edge and follow their conscience without much regard for the social acceptability of their mission. The force that drives them is their need to do something as a tribute to their son or daughter, along with the belief that their actions may prevent other tragedies.

Many grievers also find that they no longer run away from those who have experienced a personal loss. Knowing a lot more about ongoing grief, I understand as never before the importance of ongoing care and concern. Post-loss I am much more likely to take the time and make the effort to reach out with hugs, calls, letters, visits, e-mails, voice mails, or symbolic gifts (such as flowers or candles). I regret that I had to learn the hard way how much compassionate support warms and comforts hurting hearts, including my own—not only in the immediate months following the death, but over the long haul.

The bottom line: To my surprise, I discovered that from either within myself or outside of myself I was able to summon up the courage and strength I needed to survive. Taking it one day at a time, I was astounded when I realized that those first numbing weeks and months had evolved into years. Even on those days I've woken up thinking, "I've had enough of this. I can't do this grief management thing one more day," the blessing of living through enough years having these tough days has convinced me I will make it.

There are numerous activities or strategies that help bereaved parents get through the tough days. Time and again, getting on the treadmill has helped me generate the energy I need to get my day started. For some, journaling, reading or praying get them moving while others seek out a friend or treat themselves to a favorite comfort food. Still others find solace in activities such as running, playing the piano, or hitting tennis balls against the backboard.

It has become abundantly clear that there is no quick fix when life has been shattered to the core. And while there may be moments when it seems like it would be easier to give up or quit, bereaved parents are typically able to tap into a reservoir of emotional, mental, and spiritual resiliency that they never knew existed within their being. Having endured and prevailed over circumstances that are beyond any other event previously experienced or imagined usually gives rise to the belief that they can face whatever else may be in their future.

DON'T QUIT

When things go wrong
As they tragically will,

When the road you're trudging
Seems all uphill,

When all seems empty and dark
And the journey is long,

When spirits are low
And you don't feel strong,

When grief is getting
You down more than a bit,

Whatever else you do,
Don't you quit!

When your life has been
Turned inside out,

When questions abound
Among clouds of doubt,

It's on those days
Angels may be near

To lift you up
When these words you hear,

"Just stick to the fight
When you're hardest hit—

It's when things seem bleakest
That you mustn't quit!"

ADAPTED FROM AUTHOR UNKNOWN

THERE'S MORE TO GRIEF THAN THE "EYE CAN SEE"

Throughout life, there are any number of loss experiences—loss of personal possessions and relationships, loss of dreams and goals, loss of a familiar environment, loss of the ability to function mentally, emotionally, or physically, as well as numerous losses related to the developmental stages in life—that vary greatly in emotional intensity.

Yet the words that commonly permeate conversations about loss, such as "healing," "recovery," "resolution," and "closure," have not acknowledged this variability. Instead, they seemingly prescribe a progression that will inevitably lead to the conclusion of the grieving process. An editorial written by Ellen Goodman titled "Let's Add Closure to All of This Talk About Healing," (Boston Globe, 1998) lamented the unrealistic expectation society has for "healing" and "closure" regardless of the intensity level of a specific loss. The editorial observed how the bereaved may sense that they are failing to grieve properly if cultural expectations for "healing" and "closure" are not met in a timely manner.

Shortly after Erik's and David's deaths I became aware of these same expectations. Even though these words were intended to offer hope and comfort, they sank like a rock in the pit of my stomach. As defined in the dictionary, the synonyms for "heal" include "cured" and "made whole"; "recovery" means "to return to a normal condition;" and "resolution" and "closure" refer to "a conclusion or ending point."

It took almost eight years before I finally figured out that my strong reaction to these words was related to the feeling of being pushed onto a healing treadmill. Just as we're used to fast food, fast lines, fast photo finishing, and fast computers, the implication is that grieving, too, will move at a similarly fast pace. Many bereaved parents sense an expectation that their mourning period should last no longer than a year, give or take a few months. In other words, at about the same time shock is giving way to the full brunt of the mental, spiritual, and emotional turmoil, the bereaved are getting the implicit or explicit message that it is time to close the book on their grief, even though just a few pages have been written.

How could I possibly meet this high standard? I could not, and still cannot, begin to conceive of being healed from a loss that has changed the essence of who I am. I could not imagine reverting back to being my "old self" again, just as an amputee could not imagine being able to grow his leg or arm back in place. I felt as if I was destined to fail at grieving.

In contrast, when a tornado pummeled our community, experts in natural disaster recovery cautioned us not to expect too much too soon. We were told time and time again that it would take a minimum of three to five years before all the rebuilding, repairs, and replanting would be completed. As rebuilding efforts began, it became apparent that it was going to take at least that long to replace or restore the thousand-plus buildings, repair miles of sidewalks and streets, and complete improvements in the water and electrical systems. Moreover, decades of years, in some cases more than a lifetime, would be needed before the thousands of newly planted trees would reach the height and breadth of the largest trees uprooted in the storm.

Seeing the damage firsthand contributed to an understanding of the havoc that could be inflicted on a community. Visitors traveling through or into our city could see all the construction that was going on and think, "Wow, the progress that has been made in rebuilding in just a few months is remarkable!" But those who took time to look deeper would see that the community continued to look "beat up," and that the job of rebuilding was just beginning. Seeing for themselves contributed mightily to an understanding of the magnitude of the damage and the fact that it was going to take time—a long time—to recover from the devastation.

How is it that a five-year "recovery" period following a tornado is considered to be well within the normal range, but taking more than a year to "recover" from the death of a child is outside the normal limits? How could I turn my seemingly Mission Impossible into Mission Possible?

A physical wound is frequently and conveniently used as a metaphor for a grief wound. As a common, everyday experience, small physical wounds such as cuts and scrapes typically heal quickly and smoothly—within days or a couple of weeks at most. Does this metaphor contribute to the expectation that grief wounds will routinely heal in a matter of weeks or months and only rarely take a full year?

As a nurse, I also knew that this healing business is not always what it is cracked up to be. Healing can be really messy. While fairly rare, infected wounds can ooze gooey, gunky green pus with an extremely pungent odor (enough to make a person with a weak stomach throw up—I've come close). Other wounds known as chronic stasis ulcers, generally on the leg, can remain open and, despite the best of care, can become infected. And in extreme situations, amputation of the limb is needed to prevent a systemic infection and possible death.

It is my belief that grief wounds show this same variability. Some grief wounds heal quickly with no scarring, others result in scarring of varying degrees, while those experiencing a catastrophic loss work to adjust to living with an open wound that is symbolic of shadow grief.

In addition, are these different expectations for "recovery" also connected to the difference between being able to see the devastation from a natural disaster with one's own eyes and not being able to see the internal devastation that occurs in one's entire being—body, mind, and spirit—following the death of a child? Does this *unseen nature of grief* make it more difficult to understand how grief resulting from a catastrophic loss could change the core of one's inner self?

So what, exactly, is the timetable for grieving? Even though theorists have emphasized over and over that there is no defined time frame for grief resolution, the fact that most theories identify a set number of stages in the grieving process carries with it the implication that there must be an ending, since the actual loss event had a specific beginning. Following that logical line of thinking, the likely assumption is that in time, grief resolution is a predestined outcome regardless of the intensity level of the loss.

How, then, can the assertion that grieving is open-ended be reconciled with the expectation that the grieving process, once begun, should end at some defined time? In order to mentally juggle these concepts to fit together with each other, it might reasonably be assumed that one's experience with personal grief wounds will determine one's own timetable for grief resolution.

It would also appear reasonable to assume that grief wounds with a moderate intensity level tend to become the benchmark for grief resolution, since relatively few of life's losses are likely to fall outside this intensity level of pain. Given this, it would take a loss by death of a higher intensity level, with its more intense emotional pain, to reset the timetable to a longer span of time, implicitly acknowledging that previous expectations for grief resolution are now too limited.

And so it was with me. Prior to the deaths of my sons, the same ingrained assumptions and conventional view of grief had resulted in my thinking that grief was resolved in relatively short order without any significant or sustained wear and tear on one's soul. Now I understood, as I never could have before, how acute grief can transition into ongoing grief that can possibly be lifelong. Unfortunately, I had to experience that depth of emotional pain before I understood that *there was more to grief than my eyes could see.*

Since others cannot *see* the impact that a specific loss, of any intensity level, has on an individual, and assuming they have not had a comparable experience, what words would be more likely to avoid making erroneous assumptions about *what cannot not be seen?*

Just as there are words that "push" for a specific outcome, other words communicate to the bereaved that they have permission to mourn. For instance, in acknowledging acts of kindness that have warmed my heart, the word "comforting" would be more descriptive of that experience than the ubiquitous word "healing." Similarly, describing an activity that has brought a renewed focus or purpose in life as being "meaningful" would tend to be more on the mark than suggesting that "recovery" was at hand. The potential for experiences that are comforting or meaningful is significant, even though my grief wound has remained open and has continued to erupt with active bleeding over the years.

As it became possible to resume a level of functioning that resulted in responsibilities being fulfilled most of the time, the word "resolution" might have been used to indicate that the grief wound was well on its way to being closed. Rather, the likely reality, when mourning continued to consume a certain amount of available energy on any given day, was that I was working hard to readjust or integrate grief into my life.

By giving the bereaved permission to mourn, these alternative words open the process by avoiding the implication that there is an implicit or explicit timeline. By steering clear of words that push for an outcome, another benefit is that the potential for feeling guilt and/or shame for continuing to grieve is lessened. These gifts give the bereaved some breathing room and also invite the possibility of entering into a meaningful discussion about the *unseen nature of grief.* Once expressed, those feelings can be acknowledged and accepted as reflecting one's current reality.

So how long does grieving take? It takes as long as it takes. And if it happens to take the rest of one's life, so be it. To illustrate, on the tenth anniversary of the bomb explosion that killed all 259 persons on the Pan Am flight over Lockerbie, Scotland, a bereaved parent observed that this anniversary was seen by some as an opportunity to bring "closure" to his tragedy. He went on to say that "closure" would come for him only when the lid on his coffin was "closed." He obviously believed he would feel the pain and grieve for his daughter for the rest of his life. Has this parent failed at grieving? Not in my book! To the contrary, this bereaved parent has likely been trying his level best to manage, or live with, his ongoing grief in ways that bring meaning and purpose to his life.

Great strides could be made if it were acknowledged that grief, as a social condition, can potentially last a lifetime when experienced as a catastrophic loss. With this adjustment in thinking, learning how to live with grief over the long haul could become an acceptable alternative to grief resolution. Add appropriate support to the picture and the basic framework would be in place to begin to make the transition from Mission Impossible to Mission Possible.

*There is no more
ridiculous custom
than the one
that makes you
express sympathy
once and for all
on a given day
to a person whose
sorrow will endure
as long as his life.*

*Such grief,
felt in such a way
is always present.
It is never to late
to talk about it,
never repetitious
to mention it
again.*

MARCEL PROUST

BUILDING A NEW SELF I:
A SAFE PLACE TO GRIEVE

Following Erik's and David's deaths, I felt stripped of the emotional supports or infrastructure that had previously provided guidance and direction for my life. Similar to Humpty Dumpty, who couldn't be put together again after his great fall, the pieces of my old self couldn't be put back together after a great loss.

What, I wondered, would be the appropriate emotional supports for my new self? My search ultimately led to the conclusion that this new infrastructure needed to have four emotional cornerstones: having a safe place to grieve, continuing to have connections with my sons, finding meaning in living, and learning how to live with my new self.

The first emotional cornerstone acknowledged up front the importance of having a safe place to grieve. This was an eye-opener to me. With all my other life losses (which my old self had perceived as being of high intensity), the thought that I would continue to need a safe place to grieve for an undetermined length of time had never entered my mind. Now, as a bereaved parent, being able to retreat to a safe place has become the anchor of my revised emotional infrastructure.

What qualifies as a safe place varies from person to person. Many find safety in being with someone who can be trusted with one's vulnerability; someone who will listen to personal feelings and thoughts with unconditional acceptance; someone who understands the importance of confidentiality. At other times, safety may be found in spending time alone in a peaceful setting, such as at home, in a chapel, park or garden, or by a grave site, to reflect, pray, or meditate. Some find specific activities helpful. Writing has given me a safe place to go with my grief and, at the same time, has helped me process and articulate loss-related concepts. Others find activities such as keeping a journal, painting, music, or sculpting give them a meaningful way to express their grief and love.

While many find support through professional counseling or group therapy sessions, countless others find it helpful to participate in a self-help group for bereaved parents. An indicator of the intensity and duration of parental grief is seen in the number of national organizations that have been initiated at the grass roots level by bereaved parents. The primary mission of these groups is to provide a safe place in which to sort out personal reactions to their child's death and/or advocate for social change. Some are organized around the specific issues confronting parents when their child has, for example, been murdered, died of SIDS (Sudden Infant Death Syndrome), been killed by a drunk driver, or died by suicide. Some find groups helpful in the acute phase of grieving; others attend in the chronic phase or both phases; some participate for weeks, others for months or years.

More than four years into our grief journey, my husband and I became connected with The Compassionate Friends, a self-help group for bereaved parents and siblings. This organization has nearly 600 chapters in the United States with a presence in an estimated twenty-nine countries around the world. While the primary way for most bereaved parents to become linked with this organization is by attending chapter meetings, we began our involvement by attending the national conference and subscribing to the magazine, *We Need Not Walk Alone*. Most recently, many others have become connected through the Web site, **www.compassionatefriends.com**.

As a newly bereaved parent attending a Compassionate Friends meeting for the first time, it could be easy to think, "What am I doing here? These are just a bunch of 'old grievers.' " Even though many have continued to need a safe place to go with their grief ten, twenty, or more years after their children had died, their purpose in continuing their participation has likely broadened over time. In being seasoned grievers they have committed themselves to a mission of walking alongside the newly bereaved on their grief journey. Besides standing with those who are taking their first painful steps on the grief road, these "seasoned grievers" continue to hang in there with them over the years until the new grievers eventually become seasoned grievers themselves.

In fact, many bereaved parents discover that their most reliable source of support over time is other bereaved parents. By having felt the intensity of parental grief, their support tends to be more comforting than well-meaning support from those who may say the right words but have not felt it. I remember with gratitude a bereaved mom who shored me up at a difficult time, when there was a particularly steep emotional mountain staring me in the face. On the day I called her, she was there for me. As I continued my walk with grief, having someone available on an "as needed" basis to stand by me and with me, gave me the gift of knowing that I need not walk alone.

Many grievers find their loss experience affirmed by seeking out grief-related materials, including books, articles, poetry, tapes, or videos, that give them an opportunity of choosing what to read, listen to, when and for how long. Setting their own pace is frequently the option chosen by those who prefer grieving by themselves or have found themselves basically alone with their grief.

Because bereaved parents vary greatly in their choice of what printed or visual resources are most helpful, a variety of resources are needed to address the many issues encountered on the grief road. It may be coincidence, but the books that have been most helpful to me were written by women, whereas the books preferred by my husband were generally written by men. Perhaps that is not so unusual after all, as perceptions are significantly influenced by gender. Other factors that are likely to influence personal reactions may include the child's age, cause of death, and one's personality type and/or belief system.

By encouraging reflection, grieving alone or with a group allows the bereaved to work through their feelings and thoughts. Equally important, personal thoughts and feelings are likely to be validated. In reading about parental grief, I discovered that I had few unique thoughts. While this was somewhat disconcerting, it was also reassuring to know that I was not alone or crazy in what I was thinking and feeling. In fact, knowing that my feelings and thoughts were not all that different from other bereaved parents has been, to say the least, affirming.

At some point in my grief journey, I came to understand that a vital part of my new self was accepting, once and for all, that I was a bereaved parent and that there would be no getting "over it." The ongoing nature of grief and pain would be similar to living with many other chronic conditions that usually do not get better with time. Similar to those who must learn to live with diabetes, a speech deficit, or any kind of disability or ongoing condition, grievers are faced with a similar challenge. The primary difference is that instead of taking medications, eating smarter, exercising more, or becoming a nonsmoker, bereaved parents benefit most from having a safe place to grieve.

Since grieving continues to be a work in progress—hard work— exploring a variety of grief survival strategies gives bereaved parents the freedom or permission to find out what does or does not work for them. Given the options and the time, they are typically connected with an appropriate resource, sometimes by choice, sometimes by trial and error, sometimes by happenstance, and sometimes by what appears to be "angelic" intervention—that is, the appropriate resource appears almost mysteriously or mystically at a time of need. How they are ultimately linked to a resource is not important; what is important is that the connection is made.

The support generated from being in a safe place is directly connected with permission to mourn. One cannot not exist without the other. Together, these two supportive forces can go a long way in nurturing the hope, courage, and strength needed to focus one's efforts and energies on learning how to live with loss.

Please hear of my lost love.
Nothing you can do will
make it all better.
Nothing you can say will
make the hurt go away.
So just listen while I tell
you of the significance of a love
that left a hole in my heart.

DOUG MANNING
INSIGHT-BOOKS, INC.

BUILDING A NEW SELF II:
CONTINUING CONNECTIONS
AND FINDING MEANING

The next two cornerstones have become the bread and butter of my revised emotional infrastructure. The bread has been maintaining meaningful connections with my sons, whereas the butter has been finding some meaning in my adversity.

Continuing Connections: When it comes to the death of a loved one, society has promoted the idea that "letting go" or disconnecting oneself from the relationship is a sign of healthy or successful grieving. This is in contrast to the many ways people strive to maintain connections to people or places that have become a part of their past. As an example, following graduation many alumnni continue to wear sweatshirts with their school or college's logo on them because it represents a connection to an important part of their life. In order to maintain a connection with their roots, perhaps their hometown, people may subscribe to the local newspaper after they have moved away. In recent years, many farmers have had to accept the hard reality that farming can no longer be their primary source of income and have begun working at "off the farm" jobs; but in order to keep the connection to the land that has been in their family for generations, it is often rented out rather than sold.

Yet when it comes to grief, the bereaved are often advised to "let go" and "move on." Working extensively with bereaved parents, Klass (1993) found that breaking the bonds with a deceased child is not an appropriate standard for their grief experience. Instead, supporting bereaved parents in their efforts to incorporate their children into their lives in a different way than when they were alive is more likely to meet their needs and comfort them.

Being encouraged to find creative ways of maintaining the relationship with my sons was a much more sensitive and hopeful message then being told I should "let go." I have become convinced that the bond a parent has with a child does not break or even begin to bend with death. My love for my children will be forever. While my relationship with them has obviously changed as a result of their deaths, they will always be part of my family and my life. Once a parent always a parent.

Periodically linking up with Erik and David's young adult friends has been an important living link to them. Since I can no longer see my sons, hear their voices, or touch them, being able to connect with their friends is about as close as my new self can get to them. More important, they have consistently given me a safe place to talk about Erik and David.

Some parents choose to wear their child's clothes, play their favorite songs, or use their personal items as a way of staying connected with them. Others begin a specific ritual—such as placing flowers on the table, lighting a candle each evening, or placing items at the grave site—that symbolizes how their child's spirit is still an essential part of their lives. Investing in public memorials, including scholarships, tree plantings, awards, or personal tributes in the local paper on the death date, is meaningful to many. Others have included their sons or daughters in their lives by "talking" to them or, as some would say, "praying" to them.

Some bereaved parents incorporate their children's causes, beliefs, or values into their lifestyle as a way of taking up where their children left off, in ways that may be contrary to anything they have done before. They may surprise themselves when they begin running, biking, volunteering for youth programs, coaching a team, or mentoring a child. Whatever the activity, it likely represents some kind of connection to their child. Erik had been committed to a physical conditioning program for years. I decided to incorporate that value into my lifestyle and was transformed, amazingly, from a confirmed couch potato into a disciplined exerciser.

My other son, David, played tennis in high school. Prior to one of his matches, I told him that I would watch him play, but that I would not be able to stay until all the matches were completed. He emphatically responded, "Mom, if you can't watch the whole team play then you shouldn't watch me play either—you support me best when you support the team." David always tried to have the last word (he loved a good debate), but in this instance there was no contest; David had the last word hands down. He went on to coach varsity tennis at a rival high school. When his team came to our community after his death, I remembered his lesson. He could not be physically present for his team, but I could.

The sharing of stories and compiling of written memories or pictures is a tried-and-true way of continuing the bond—one that can also help others learn about the deceased child. It has been meaningful to hear my grandchildren talk about and ask questions about their Uncle Erik and Uncle David. Even though they have no memory of them, their uncles are becoming part of their lives—certainly not in the way I would have preferred, but through stories and rituals they are learning to know them. Derik, born four months after his uncles' deaths, was named for both of them—a powerful, lifelong connection.

Other grievers find meaning in using their talents, such as woodworking, handwork, drawing, or writing songs, to commemorate the life of their son or daughter. These creative efforts tend to be linked with some aspect of their child's personality, philosophy of life, or social or recreational interests. Certain tributes, such as poetry, may be kept private or given as gifts to those special people who had a significant influence on their child's life. Still others choose to go public with songs, paintings, or sculptures because their message affirms and/or reflects the grief experience of many bereaved parents.

Engaging in activities that represent a connection to their child may result in the feeling that something positive and constructive is being done to honor their son or daughter. In addition to restoring a measure of meaning and purpose to their lives, these activities may also have the benefit of providing a socially acceptable outlet for grief expression.

Finding Meaning: As a bereaved parent and psychologist, Kagan (Klein)(1998) concluded that a turning point in parental bereavement occurs when parents, despite their deep sadness, begin to search for a mission. For some, the cause of their child's death becomes an immediate catalyst for their search for meaning; for others, their goals take shape gradually and evolve over time—years, in fact.

While many missions involve being more sensitive to others experiencing intense grief, many others are directly related to the cause of a child's death. The cause of the death—accident, suicide, illness, murder, or Sudden Infant Death Syndrome—often becomes the impetus for many bereaved parents to invest huge amounts of time and energy participating in organizations or projects that work towards preventing similar tragedies.

As examples, parents of children who have died by suicide may get involved in SA/VE, an organization that has educated countless others about depression; a grief-stricken mom, whose daughter was killed by a drunk driver, became the driving force behind MADD (Mother's Against Drunk Drivers); and a devastated dad went on a crusade to change the laws regarding violent sex offenders. The actions of persistent and determined parents, actively lobbying for change, has resulted in legislation that has saved lives, protected victims, and/or stiffened consequences for offenders.

The accomplishment of many goals frequently requires grant writing or fund-raising of some kind. Most fund-raising events sponsored in memory of a loved one, such as an art show, cross-country run, concert, fishing contest, or sports tournament, typically take place at the local community level. While these events successfully generate media attention and financial support for a worthwhile cause, what makes them meaningful for bereaved parents is the connection with their loved one.

By seeking out organizations that share their vision of what actions need to be taken in order to make this world a better place, these parents begin to sense that their life continues to have a purpose. The energy that comes from a passion born out of deep sadness has frequently yielded impressive results.

Other missions, seemingly unconnected to their loved one, may in fact be directly connected. The daughter of a bereaved parent couple loved animals. While horses were her passion, another of her dreams was to have a family-operated dairy farm. Following her death, her parents took a significant financial risk to bring this dream to fruition. Their sense that their daughter's spirit is cheering them on and working alongside them has given their lives a purpose that goes well beyond the basic need to generate an income.

Regarding my mission, my gut told me that if I was going to go on living, I needed to find some meaning in my adversity. In order to rebuild my new self following my sons' deaths, many of my old self's priorities were either removed from my "What's Really Important for Life" list or shuffled around and reordered. In fact, my old self's pursuit might have been titled "In Pursuit of Happiness" or "In Pursuit of the Good Life." Other common pursuits prior to a catastrophic loss might have been, for example, the search for social status, wealth, power, or winning the "big one."

To have any meaning, it was essential that my mission have a strong connection to my sons. My initial goal (along with my husband) was to use insurance monies and memorials to establish several scholarships and other tributes carrying Erik and David's name. Shortly after their deaths we framed literally hundreds of copies of David's signature quote (see page 4) and the Walk in the World piece (see page 185) to give to their friends. Then, over the next few years, I cross-stitched a number of handmade gifts for those who had been a significant influence in their lives.

About two years after the accident I began writing to other bereaved parents. Even though there was nothing I could say or do to diminish their sadness, I could acknowledge their emotional pain and their never-ending love for their child, and give them permission to mourn. Later I began to speak up publicly through letters to the editor and radio interviews regarding The Compassionate Friends Worldwide Candle Lighting memorial.

Then I began writing essays. I will be the first to say that prior to my sons' deaths, I did not readily sit down to write except as part of my job responsibilities. So it was rather surprising when writing became the survival strategy that, in large part, made it possible to keep on going on, especially on those tough emotional days. Giving voice to my grief experience has, in essence, become integral to my pursuit for meaning.

I could have never imagined that my walk with grief would take me in the direction it did. It just more or less evolved. Even though I have no idea where my mission will take me in the future, I'm convinced that it will be the major driving force as I continue on with my life—living still and loving always.

Rita's sweet son Adam took up her time.
Caregiving for Pamela Sue occupied mine.
Now, Pam and Adam are tragically gone.
They left us, their mothers, to try to go on.

We talk and we cry, we think what to do
To live with just memories, so sad and so true.
Her loss is my loss, her pain is mine.
She hopes for justice, I pray for time.

We'll work in their memories, we'll open the doors,
Put crooks behind bars, raise money for cures.
Meetings and rallies will fill up our lives,
Two mothers who love two children who died.

ADAPTED FROM SANDRA M. CHAIKEN
BEREAVEMENT MAGAZINE
SEPTEMBER/OCTOBER, 1999

Another essential assumption of this model holds that regaining a sense of stability or balance is not the conclusion of the grieving process. Rather, the reality is that at any time and any place, any experience, expected or unexpected, can knock the new self out of balance over and over again. This appears to be consistent with Knapp's assertion that under certain circumstances and on certain occasions, the fairly constant emotional dullness of shadow grief will come bubbling to the surface. However it's described, Kagan (Klein) theorizes that readjustment, or the taking of inward and outward steps during recurring periods of imbalance, is a lifelong process.

This model gave me permission to toss all those unrealistic expectations for a grieving deadline into the wastebasket. It was comforting to know that my new self had the freedom of taking the rest of my life, if necessary, to readjust to my radically changed reality. I came to recognize that stability in functioning was linked to being able to bounce back from periods of imbalance, which more accurately described the fluidity and unpredictability of the parental grief experience. I no longer felt as if I was failing at grieving.

With this perspective, finding ways to accommodate or integrate grief into their new selves' "normal" becomes a major component of many bereaved parents' readjustment. The options chosen reflect each individual's unique grief experience. Continuing to incorporate their son or daughter into their family's life through meaningful connections is the choice of many. For some, recognizing that ongoing grief is similar to any other life-changing or chronic health condition that can be managed helps them regain a sense of balance. An important facet of readjustment for others is figuring out how to connect with a mission that provides a sense of meaning and purpose. Then there are those who find it important to identify new priorities, values, beliefs, and assumptions that are a better fit with their revised worldview.

It cannot be assumed that the task of defining one's new self has been completed once the emotional cornerstones for the infrastructure have been laid. In fact, the task has just begun. Just as a road needs continuous and ongoing maintenance, the new self constructed around the holes and cracks in one's life also needs ongoing and continuous refurbishing.

It would be hard to imagine what could possibly have a more significant impact on one's changed life than continuing to give and receive the gift of unconditional love—lots of it. By providing the glue that forms the solid base for one's new self and by being the catalyst for generating a sense of hope, courage, and strength, love cannot be assigned a value. When it is experienced, it is priceless.

FOREVER CHANGED

Can you see the change in me?
It may not be so obvious to you.

I participate in family activities. I attend family reunions.
I help plan the holiday meals.
You tell me you're glad to see that I don't cry any more.

But I do cry. When everyone is gone—when it is safe—the tears fall.
I cry in privacy so my family won't worry.
I cry until I am exhausted and can finally sleep.

I'm active in my church. I sing the hymns.
I listen to the sermon. You tell me you admire my strength
and my positive attitude.

But I'm not strong. I feel that I have lost control,
and I panic when I think about tomorrow...next week...
next month...next year.

I go about the routine of my job. I complete my assigned tasks.
I drink coffee and smile. You tell me you're glad to see I'm "over"
the death of my loved one.

But I'm not "over" it. If I get over it, I will be the same as before
my loved one died. I will never be the same. The pain of losing
someone I love so much has left a gap too big to ever be filled.

I visit my neighbors.
You tell me you're glad to see I'm holding up so well.

But I'm not holding up well.
Sometimes I want to lock my door and hide from the world.

I spend time with friends. I appear calm and collected.
I smile when appropriate.
You tell me it's good to see me back to my "old self."

But I will never be back to my "old self."
Grief has become part of my life, and I am forever changed.

Adapted from Rhonda Wilson

WHEN LOVE IS NO LONGER TAKEN FOR GRANTED

Just months before the accident, Erik saw me crocheting and asked, "When are you going to make *me* an afghan, Mom?" And I, with all my mom wisdom, said, "Don't worry. I'll make you an afghan. I'll have *years* to make you all kinds of afghans!" Little did I know when I made that glib statement that I would have only a few months to make either Erik or David anything. I was obviously taking their lives, and my own, for granted. Some time later Erik noticed I was crocheting and teased, "Making me my afghan?" It was, in fact, his afghan, and since it was going to be a Christmas gift, I ignored his question. Now my hope has been that my silence told him that he had guessed right.

It was so easy to take my sons' lives for granted prior to their deaths. After all, each of my sons emerged from high school unscathed. My next safety milestone was college graduation. They made it, and I thought I had it made. Then we began to experience the blessings of relating to our sons as young adults. I thought it was just the best. And even though they were living in other communities, their voices were just a phone call away.

As a young mom, I remember thinking that my parenting role would be more or less "over" when my sons graduated from college. It didn't take long for me to realize that the parenting role is, instead, a work in progress—one that continued to evolve as my children moved from one developmental stage to another. When they assumed full responsibility for their lives in the young adult years, the parenting role did not end, as I had once surmised would happen, it just went through another transformation. In this stage my husband and I seemed to become supportive consultants who also just happened to be their parents.

The consultations varied from the trivial, "Mom, how do I bake a turkey?" or "When do I plant what vegetable in the garden?" to weightier issues. When David was in the process of buying a house, he asked us to come to check out his options with him. When Erik was struggling with whether or not to change career directions, he reviewed the pros and cons with us several times before he got down to the nitty-gritty of making the decision. We felt so fortunate that the distance factor allowed us to help them on an "as needed" basis. Most of the time that meant hauling their "stuff" from one location to another.

While distance frequently separates parents from their adult children, as long as life continues, it is possible to connect with them—by sight, voice, or touch—perhaps not as often as one would wish or hope for, but at a frequency that is certainly preferable to never. Bereaved parents are confronted with having no choice but to learn to live with the "neverness" of the loss—never seeing their children again, never hearing their voices, never touching them. Well into the second year of his grief journey, one bereaved parent, grasping the finality that there would be no end to the never, said, "Now I know what 'forever' really means."

Prior to my sons' deaths, that kind of finality would have been inconceivable, incomprehensible—impossible to imagine, much less describe. The words of Wolterstorff (1987), reflecting on the death of his son, strike at the heart of the matter: "All I can do is *remember* him. I can't *experience* him." Without any new experiences that result in new memories, there is no going back, no starting over, no changing what is. And while I treasure a countless number of memories and stories, I also know that at any time, any memory or connection can engulf me with the stark and unforgiving finality

90

of their deaths. The constant presence of their absence has been unrelenting.

It was the things I had taken for granted that I have missed so much. For instance, when they were young adults I never knew when I would hear the door open and hear the hearty voice of one of my sons call out, "Hi, Mom—I'm hooome!" It was a wonderful moment that let me know that they liked to surprise me with their homecoming. Not long after that, I would hear the refrigerator door open and again hear them call out, "What's to eat?" Not being able to hear their voices again or see David's incredible smile or Erik's winning grin, along with not being able to experience countless other "normals," has contributed immensely to my grief.

Literally every memory connected to one's son or daughter, from the mundane to the momentous, the high points and the low points, will likely become part of the parental grief experience. The simple rhythms of a normal day, which had been sources of delight, irritation, or stress, are all grieved—perhaps the foods they loved, the music they listened to, the clothes they wore or didn't wear, or their messy rooms.

Kagan (Klein) (1998) wisely noted that a child's death also keeps bereaved parents from experiencing the "normal" life crises that frequently accompany parenthood. These normal crises would range from the worrisome (such as not keeping curfew, difficulty with money management, or not liking their child's choice of friends) to the potentially life-threatening (such as choosing values and exhibiting behaviors that threatened their health and safety). Given the option, bereaved parents would willingly take on those "normal" life crises again, even though it would be difficult, because it would mean their child was still alive.

Another factor that contributes mightily to parental grief is the hard reality that their child will never have the option of experiencing all of the milestones typically experienced in a lifetime. While bereaved parents grieve the loss of the dreams and goals they had for their children, more significantly they grieve the loss of dreams and goals their children had, or would have had, for themselves. Dreaming about all the possibilities and then making plans to make those dreams come true is often the primary compass determining the direction of the future. I would venture to say that most of us have no idea how big an influence our hopes, dreams, and goals for the future actually have had on our life until that future is no more.

I never thought much about any of this until after my sons' deaths. I just took it for granted that there would be another phone call, another visit, that I would help launch Erik on his career as a physical therapist, that I would have years of watching David coach tennis and would share in their lives as they became proud fathers. I never realized, to the extent that I do now, how each day with them alive was such an incredible gift—that loving them alive was the greatest of all gifts.

Another one of the many lessons I learned about life after loss was that my love for my sons basically stood alone as a feeling as long as they were alive. Grief and emotional pain changed all that. It was only when their deaths resulted in my love becoming welded to the emotional pain that I became aware of just how deep and wide my love was for them.

From that point on, I knew beyond the shadow of a doubt that their deaths would never change the fact that I would always be Erik and David's mom. A prime example occurred when the local paper omitted Erik's name, not once but twice, when announcing the recipient of the Erik and David Aasen Leadership Award. The first time it happened I dismissed it as a typographical error, but when it happened a second time a line had been crossed and I reached for the phone. It felt soooo good to say, "I'm Nita Aasen, and I'm calling as a MOM."

There has been nothing so affirming as the times I am approached and asked, "Are you by any chance David (or Erik or Kevin)

Aasen's mom?" And with a tremendous sense of gratitude and always using the present tense for each of my three sons, I have answered, *"YES, I AM!"*

Only the person who is incapable of love
is entirely free of the possibility of grief.

In the words of a dying man:
"The agony is great and yet I will stand it.
Had I not loved so very much, I would not hurt so much.
But goodness knows, I would not want
to diminish the precious love by one fraction.
I will hurt and I will be grateful for it.
For it bears witness to the depth of our meanings
and for that I will be eternally grateful."

SCOTTY, HOSPICE CHAPLAIN
"FOREVER REMEMBERED," 1997
COM-PEN-DI-UM, INC.
SEATTLE, WA

THE SILENCE SURROUNDING
LOSS AND GRIEF

Bereaved parents tend to feel left out of the conversation loop when their children's lives have stopped in time. It didn't take long before I was confronted with the harsh reality that my sons' lives, their entire lives were in the past, a history that tended to be encircled with silence. In talking with others about the silence surrounding loss and grief, a lot of *if only's* were mentioned. *If only* the loss would be acknowledged, *if only* I could talk about my grief, *if only* something would be said about my child.

Many refrain from saying "something" to bereaved parents because they think this would add to the pain. Conversely, in taking the risk of bringing their child's name into a conversation, many bereaved parents become aware of an awkward silence, a stiffening in the body language, or a nonverbal flinch. And if years have gone by without hearing their son's or daughter's name spoken, it may feel as if he or she had never been alive. Very quickly, the fear that their child has been forgotten may become all too real.

This is not as far fetched as it may sound. In a promotional effort to create awareness of the Worldwide Candle Lighting Memorial in our local communities, bereaved parents were invited to have their child's name included in a remembrance list. A bereaved mom, her voice trembling, shared that it had been more than thirty years since her child had died and an unknown number of years since she had said his name out loud. Now the Worldwide Candle Lighting event was giving her permission and a reason to break the silence and say his name out loud. She couldn't have received a more meaningful gift.

This begs the question: What is behind all this silence surrounding loss and grief? One of the most commonly heard expressions of sympathy from friends, coworkers, and extended family members are the words, "I'm so sorry to hear about your loss." And then the subject is frequently changed.

Prior to my sons' deaths, I was also one of those who confined most condolences to those few words. Many times, regardless of the intensity level of the loss, those words essentially began and ended the conversation about their loved one. And there were other times when I said nothing to acknowledge the death. In not saying "something" at a minimum, I ignored the loss completely. And the silence began.

But what happens when someone breaks a bone or needs surgery? The ill or injured are deluged with questions: "What happened? Where were you? Were you alone? How soon can you go running again?" Over and over they are invited to tell their story, and the more specific the details the better. Then there are the follow up questions: "How's the arm coming along? Are you still having pain? How are you sleeping? How has it affected your tennis game?" Tons of questions. There is a bubble of verbal concern that surrounds the person. The strong arm of social support envelops and comforts them.

Perhaps what makes it easier to ask questions about fixable or controllable health conditions, such as broken bones or other health problems, is our extensive experience with asking those questions. From childhood on up we've had opportunities to practice these skills by asking questions about skinned knees, cuts, bruises, colds, broken bones, or the flu.

Just as happens with common health ailments, the most effective way of inviting a conversation about loss and grief is to ask questions. To illustrate, two months after my sons' deaths, two of David's friends called and asked if they could come over for an hour or so. As an introvert, I wondered what we would talk about for a whole hour. I didn't need to wonder. As soon as they came in the house, it was obvious that they were on a mission to find out what had happened on that fateful day. There was no preliminary chitchat. They got right down to the nitty-gritty. They wanted to know every detail about the accident—how our sons looked sitting lifeless in the car, what we did, how we felt, how we got through each day, and if our thinking about life, death, and an afterlife had changed. These questions, in spite of their directness, were asked with incredible caring and concern. And we were just as direct in our responses. Their questions gave us permission to tell our story with no holds barred.

This was no ordinary conversation that lasted for an hour; instead, the questions and discussion about those questions continued for more than five hours. For many of the questions there were no answers. What was so important about that evening was the gift we gave to each other of our time, our attention, and our caring so that it would be a safe place to mourn—a safe place to ask our questions. To this day, that evening, which extended into the early morning hours, stands out as one of the most meaningful experiences of my life.

Several of my sons' friends also shared how difficult it was to talk about their friend and their grief with coworkers and friends who had not had a similar experience. Even after a leading statement that literally begged to be followed up with a question, their request to have the silence broken was, with rare exceptions, ignored. It was almost as if there was an unwritten and unspoken agreement to keep the lid on grief by keeping silent about it. It was no surprise, then, that grief was not a topic that was easily substituted for talking about topics such as sports, the latest romantic interest, or weekend parties. Fortunately, these friends knew that they could break the silence with us or with mutual friends. And so they would—and still do—call, write or visit. By keeping connected with us, they are indirectly staying connected with our sons. Friends forever as they say.

I have been thankful for those occasions when others have taken the time to break the silence and have shared a memory or reflection about my sons. Here are two of those treasured gifts. Well into the fifth year after the accident, we received a letter from one of Erik's friends. In working with this friend on class projects, Erik had come to know her family quite well. In fact, her two young children always looked forward to his visits because they knew he would take time to play with them. The letter related how another bereaved parent, as a tribute to her daughter, had invited the community to run or walk in memory of someone they loved in a "Race to Remember." Since Erik had touched all their lives, it had been an easy decision for his friends to decide to run for him. In addition to the story, the letter included pictures of the family (the children almost grown up) holding the marker with Erik's name. I will be forever grateful that Erik's friend took the time and made the effort to let us know, with both words and pictures, how her family continued to remember him.

Now the story about David. Almost five years after the deaths of my sons, we received a letter from a young woman who had lived in our community as a young child. She told the story about a hot summer day when she and her friend had set up a lemonade stand. My son, about fourteen years old at the time, stopped to buy a glass of lemonade for five cents. He gave her a dollar and said, "Keep the change. It's a tip!" The girls were ecstatic with their benefactor's generosity (years later she learned it was David). Knowing how quickly my son could down a glass of lemonade, the entire interaction probably took less than five minutes. Now, years later, this young woman told us how she stops at every lemonade stand she comes across. When paying for the lemonade she gives each young entrepreneur a dollar and says, "Keep the change. It's a tip!" in honor of my son, who made her day on that hot day years ago.

What prompted this young woman to write us (she has never met us) years after the accident? I have no idea. Might she have had a debate with herself, or with others, about whether or not she should tell us the story? Possibly. Was there some hesitation as she took the time to write the letter, and did it take more than a bit of courage to drop the letter in the mailbox? Probably. But she did it! She could have given us no greater gift. To know that David's spontaneous moment of kindness had motivated her to take on that same gesture as a way of honoring and remembering him was powerful stuff. If my son knew about this, he would shake his head in disbelief and wonder how such a seemingly little thing could have possibly meant so much. But isn't that how the old adage goes? "Little things mean a lot."

Bereaved parents receive tangible evidence that their child is remembered and continues to live on in the hearts and minds of others when questions are asked about their grief journey or they hear a story about their child. Regardless of the number of years since a child's death, having the silence broken is one of those little things that is really a big thing, and it means a lot!

THE ELEPHANT IN THE ROOM

There's an elephant in the room.
It is large and squatting,
so it is hard to get around it.
Yet we squeeze by with
"How are you" and "I'm fine,"
and a thousand other forms of trivial chatter.
We talk about the weather.
We talk about work.
We talk about everything—
except the elephant in the room.

There's an elephant in the room.
We all know it's there.
We are thinking about the elephant
as we talk together.
It is constantly on our minds.
For you see, it's a very big elephant.
It has hurt us all.
But we do not talk about the
elephant in the room.

Oh please, say her name.
Oh please, say "Barbara" again.
Oh please, let's talk about the
elephant in the room.
For if we talk about her death,
perhaps we can talk about her life?
Can I say "Barbara" to you and not
have you look away?

For if I cannot, then you are leaving me
alone...
in a room...
with an elephant...

TERRY KETTERING

EMOTIONAL
MOUNTAINS

As they continue their grief journey, many bereaved parents find that certain situations trigger an emotional reaction that is too painful to manage graciously. One bereaved parent referred to these difficult situations as "emotional mountains." These mountain ranges have peaks of varying heights. Some of these peaks are scalable, while others stop one short in his or her tracks. As each situation presents itself, a decision must be made about whether or not it is worth the stress and internal turmoil to climb a particular mountain.

There is, understandably, a great deal of variability among bereaved parents in what they identify as their emotional challenges. Some mountains are encountered at home or a similar private place, where the struggle isn't directly observed. In contrast, others occur in a more public setting, where the bereaved's vulnerability is out in the open. These emotional challenges are frequently associated with the many life stages and milestones parents expected their son or daughter to experience. With traditions, special occasions, traumatic events, or ordinary daily occurrences symbolizing a connection with one's child, many mountains involve holidays, graduations, baby showers, a particular season of the year, driving past a hospital, making French toast, or sorting out a child's belongings.

There has been no steeper mountain for me to climb than the wedding mountain. Nothing has been more symbolic of the future my sons will not have than the loss of the possibility of their marrying. And while there is no way of knowing if either of them *would* have married, there is no disputing the fact that their deaths ended all their options, all their choices, all their dreams, all their goals.

Completely unaware of the emotional mountains that might be littering the bereaved's landscape, caring others may encourage them to begin doing "this" or doing "that." The reality is that they may not feel up to doing "this or that." Just like in a tug-of-war, there may be the feeling of being pushed and pulled—pushed towards accepting the request or invitation versus pulling away or escaping from an emotional mountain. Neither choice represents a win-win situation. Neither choice results in a calm gut.

In the real world there are very few invitations and requests that have a built-in "out." When there are invitations or events that make one's gut churn because the choice is an *either/or* kind of situation, the dilemma is deciding which choice will make the gut feel the most settled. Because of the push-pull tensions, much soul-searching is likely involved in making those decisions.

There were two contrasting situations involving my emotional mountain that occurred several years apart. The first occurred about two years after the accident. After being informed about an upcoming wedding, I was lobbied over the next several months with multiple reasons for attending. As I wrestled with the decision, I lacked the courage to be up-front about the reason for the struggle. Ultimately I concluded that the inner turmoil that would result from saying yes would not be worth the emotional price.

Even though I never regretted my decision not to force myself to climb that emotional mountain, I still felt guilty. So I called another bereaved mom whose daughter, Rene, had died in a car accident twelve days before Erik and David had died. She promptly told me to stop beating myself up. Over and over she said, "You don't have to go to weddings. You don't have to do that to yourself." In sharing that she had chosen not to attend the weddings of her two nieces a year earlier, she said, "Rene was engaged at the time of her death, and

I just couldn't take the flowing white gown and all that goes with it." Weddings were her emotional mountain as well. After our conversation, I knew I was not walking alone.

Thankfully, many grief-related books have addressed this dilemma by emphasizing the importance of grievers being good to themselves— of giving themselves permission to protect themselves from situations that would be inordinately painful. Given the time to consider the options for each "this or that" situation, the bereaved likely have the capacity or wherewithal to make a decision that is ultimately in the best interests of everyone. Acknowledging that reality frees them from feeling as if they need to pretend to be what they no longer are.

Now for the second situation involving my emotional mountain. Fast-forward several years. One of David's good friends came over to tell me that he would be getting married sometime within the next year. I knew he wanted me to share the event with him. This time, however, as a more seasoned griever and feeling safe, it was easier to gather up the courage and strength to say in summary, "You know that I wish you both the very best. But to be fair, I need to be up-front with you. Because there is nothing that is more visibly symbolic of the future Erik and David will never have, I have given myself permission to forego weddings." In response, he said simply and genuinely, "Thank you for telling me." Blessed acceptance and understanding! What a gift!

Although I didn't attend, I did cross-stitch and frame a piece that commemorated their marriage with their names and wedding date. In this way I could give something of myself while sending my best wishes with all of my heart and soul.

Gathering up the courage to share with others how difficult it is to climb some emotional mountains might increase the possibility that at least a few invitations or requests would be offered as a true choice, which could be freely accepted or declined. In being given some elbow room—that is, by not being backed into a corner—it may become easier for the bereaved to consider whether or not they could gather up the courage and strength to climb a specific mountain. Without any strings or conditions attached to invitations or requests and with lots of backup, the possibility of tackling some of the smaller mountains and gradually working up to some of the higher peaks may, in time, seem less risky.

Ultimately, many bereaved parents find that a major hurdle has been mastered when they can give themselves permission to decline to climb certain mountains. Once that point is reached, a decision about the feasibility of climbing a particular mountain can made that is largely independent of outside influences.

FRENCH TOAST

I stand here before the stove. All the ingredients are here,
The eggs, the milk, vanilla, cinnamon, and sugar.

The frying pan is heating slowly, melting the butter
And still I stand in my robe and slippers.

I pick up an egg to break it in the bowl, but I just can't do it.
I want so much to fix French toast because my husband loves it so.

Just like my son did all his life...Right up until he died.
I've lived this scene so many times since then,
always with a tear and a sigh.

We'd had French toast at least once a week
for more years than I can remember.
How they ate! I'd laugh and complain
because I had to cook so much.

Once, in Florida, when we had French toast
for breakfast in a restaurant with friends,
He said, "This is okay, but you ought to taste my mom's!"
I can still hear him saying it.

Now I just can't do it. I cannot cook French toast!

My husband never asks, and while I stand before the stove and weep,
he pretends not to notice. But I know he understands.

I just can't cook French toast. Not yet.

FAY HARDEN
TUSCALOOSA, ALABAMA
FOOD FOR THE SOUL
BEREAVEMENT PUBLISHING COMPANY

109

STRAIGHT TALK
OR SPIN CONTROL:
A DILEMMA

As a nurse, I thought I understood the grieving process. After all, I had completed, as well as taught, classes on death, dying, loss, and grieving. I had been with family members and their loved one facing a terminal illness. I had been present at the deaths of many patients. I had been in the emergency room when children and adults were brought in by ambulance after a fatal car accident. I had experienced personal losses. I had seen death up close and personal, or so I thought.

Then lightning struck full force when Erik and David were killed. It was on that day that I was catapulted to a level of understanding about grieving that would have been unimaginable to my old self. I realized that, prior to the accident, I hadn't had a clue about the incredible gut-wrenching emotional pain that went along with a catastrophic loss. Before the loss, as the slang expression goes, I didn't "get it." Being exposed to grieving concepts had been helpful in gaining some *knowledge* about the loss and grieving experience. But as I found out the hard way, knowledge does not equal *understanding*. They are as far apart as night and day. Actually, I'm not sure any amount of "education," either in the classroom or clinical setting, could have "prepared" me for my experience with parental grief.

My first hint of just how unprepared I was occurred when I discovered that my old self's habits for responding to everyday social occurrences no longer fit my new self. These ordinary situations had been as much a part of my life as getting up in the morning. Now I struggled with how to respond: I had to make a choice between straight talk and spin control. This dilemma could not be ignored.

The primary dilemma was that being honest was often pitted against the need for some protective cover. Whenever straight talk—being forthright about the ups and downs of my grief experience—was at odds with mainstream thinking, I felt the tension rising to the surface. Spin control, on the other hand, minimized the risk. It provided a way to play it safe, to avoid rocking the boat, to keep the peace.

Prior to the accident, I was rather surprised whenever individuals shared their personal stories—spilling their guts, so to speak—with people they were unlikely to ever see or hear from again. Now, with some personal experience under my belt, I understand how that happens. Contrary to my usual reticence, when given the opportunity to talk about parental grief, my verbosity has bordered on what might be called unbridled diarrhea of the mouth. My ideas, thoughts, and feelings about grief have literally poured out of my mouth to strangers who have given me the gift of their sensitivity and listening ear. How was it that I felt safe with a stranger? Since it was unlikely that our paths would cross again, talking to strangers involved very little risk. The anonymity of the situation protected my privacy and vulnerability. It was a safe place to engage in straight talk.

But spin control also has its benefits. Just as politicians use spin to slant a story for appearance' sake, many grievers have also sensed when it is appropriate to disguise or cover up personal thoughts and feelings. With this strategy, it may be easy to create an impression that everything is back to normal. For example, when family and friends see someone who has experienced an intense loss smiling and chatting, it becomes easy to assume that the person is back to being his or her "old self" again. Thinking they are being complimentary, they may state enthusiastically, "It's good to see you doing so well!"—totally unaware of how unnatural the very natural acts of smiling and chatting feel post-loss. Acknowledging this disparity with a straight-talk response of "It may not look like it, but I'm really having a hard time holding it together" would correct that assumption. In contrast, the question "You appear to be getting through the days quite well," but how are you really doing?" avoids making an assumption and invites a straight-talk response.

Many bereaved parents also find that spin control helps them pull themselves together so that family, work, and community obligations can be met despite their ongoing grief and pain. In other words, when their emotional state is fragile, spin control helps them get through the day. I have become quite adept at dual thinking; that is, thinking about my sons while at the same time appearing to be focused solely on the task at hand. Even though my thoughts about my sons move to the background when I am engaged in another activity or conversation, they are still there, still a part of my awareness.

And, as I learned, I am not alone. In testing her Readjustment Model of Parental Bereavement, Kagan (Klein) (*We Need Not Walk Alone, Spring, 2001*) reported that 73 percent of parents continued to think about their son or daughter "all day and every day" after the first year anniversary of their child's death. Furthermore, this intense and frequent thinking about their child was found to persist after the tenth year suggesting that this phenomenon becomes part of many bereaved parents (especially mothers) new normal.

Shortly after the accident, I also found myself encountering the nuances behind common social greetings. Lifelong habits were suddenly seen from a different perspective when I realized the primary purpose of these greetings was simply to acknowledge my presence. There was no getting around the most common greeting of all: "Hi, how are you?" When the typical response of "good" or "fine" did not fit, a more neutral reply such as "Okay" or "Not too bad" may have been the chosen spin control reply. A common response to that bland answer was often an enthusiastic "Good!" It didn't take me long to recognize that a straight-talk response of "No, not exactly," along with a detailed description about how I was "really" doing was not welcomed, so I shifted the conversation to another, safer topic — a classic spin control response.

Since recognizing that an obligatory "okay" response from those who are bereaved rarely means "A–OK," my new self has gotten into the habit of rephrasing the "how are you?" question as "On the surface you appear to be getting through the days quite well, but how are you really doing?" or "How are your days (or nights, weekends or holidays, summer or winter) going?" or "What is helping you get through the days?"

Reactions to social events following a catastrophic loss experience can also change significantly depending on individual personalities and life experiences. I'm unsure how much of my personal reaction to social situations comes from my being a strong, task-oriented introvert. I have well-developed "alone" skills. I rarely feel lonely when I'm alone. When alone, another benefit is that I feel no pressure to "go along to get along." I can just be.

Structured groups such as meetings, sports events, classes, or programs were manageable because there were issues to discuss, tasks to complete, games to watch, or problems to solve. In contrast, my discomfort at being in unstructured social groups, particularly parties and receptions, has increased in intensity. At those times when I felt that I did not fit in a situation, mustering up the energy needed to participate in a group conversation or social activity became a major spin control challenge. It was certainly possible, as I discovered, to feel both alone and lonely in social situations.

Overall, bereaved parents become quite proficient at spin — at putting on whatever socially correct face would be required at the time. Yet there are inevitably those times when an unpredictable event triggers an acute emotional response and the tears flow in a torrent. Despite well-intentioned efforts, the spin control strategy can sometimes become unglued.

I quickly learned that grief precipitated emotions that were much more powerful than any of my efforts to control them. I began referring to these occurrences as the "back door" phenomenon. While I had been able to prepare, to some extent, for scheduled "front door" events, such as a public ceremony that honored my sons, unpredictable back door events have caught me totally off guard. There was no way to prepare for these raw emotional moments, just as there would be no way to prepare for company that showed up unexpectedly at my back door. While I could not anticipate when I would be "back doored," the event became less stressful when I accepted these moments as just another one of those emotional days on the grief road when it was time to grab a Kleenex and ride it out.

By promoting an open exchange of feelings and thoughts in a safe place, straight talk offers the best chance for a win-win situation for both the bereaved and their friends and family. In being given permission to remove the spin control mask, the bereaved are more likely to feel affirmed, comforted, and loved, wherever they might be in their grief journey.

MAY I GRIEVE

In the daytime, I walk and work and all;
But at home, in the evening, I stumble and fall.
The office says, "Function, smile, get control."
But at home I can grieve to cleanse my soul.

Must I be two people for the rest of my life?
Can I make it through pain and struggle and strife?
If I could be just one person for more than one day.
My freedom to grieve would help light the way.

ADAPTED FROM SUZANNE DEMARS,
THE COMPASSIONATE FRIENDS
HINGHAM, MA

THE GIFT
OF LISTENING

I was in my middle adult years when I found myself reflecting on life and how lucky I had been not to have experienced any major catastrophes. And I wondered, "Is it possible that I'll actually go through life without experiencing some kind of tragedy?" When Erik and David were killed a few months later, I had the answer to that question in no uncertain terms. Then, more than three years later, the entire community of St. Peter, Minnesota, was struck by a full-blown tornado.

Minnesota snowstorms in March are a fact of life. But tornados? Not even a blip on the statistical radar screen. Yet, on a warmer-than-normal March day I turned on the local radio station to hear in no uncertain terms, "Anyone who lives in St. Peter, go to your basement NOW! LET'S GO!" The urgency in the broadcaster's voice was for real; this was no ordinary run-of-the-mill storm warning. Our community was in for the storm of a lifetime.

Within two minutes, a tornado wall 1.25 miles wide (normal is .25 miles wide) invaded and ravaged our town. I remember hearing incredibly noisy crashing, crunching sounds and wondering, "Why doesn't this sound like a train?" At the same time, I watched as "goodness-knows-what" went flying through the air. After the storm was over, I emerged cautiously from the basement, somewhat like a gopher coming out of his hole, and what I saw took my breath away. It looked like a war zone! Even though our house was still standing, scattered all over our yard and neighborhood was the goodness-knows-what debris—glass, shingles, bricks, uprooted trees, pieces of walls, roofs, furniture—that had hitched a ride on the ferocious tornado train as it sped through our community.

As neighbors walked the streets in stunned disbelief to verify each others safety and survey the damage, we knew we were not alone. Having experienced the same event at the same time and in the same place contributed to a powerful feeling that we were all in this together. Everyone in the community had a story to tell. For most, it meant sharing what it was like to experience the actual wrath of the tornado as it roared through town and, perhaps, through their home. Others, returning home from weekend activities, told of how they could not recognize familiar streets, instantly becoming strangers in their own small town. Landmarks had vanished from the landscape, pitch-black streets were blocked by trees, but they kept on going until they reached what may have been their former home.

Disasters are life-changing experiences for most people experiencing the full brunt of them. Most community disasters, such as a hurricane, tornado, or earthquake, fall into the "acts of nature" category and may devastate an entire community or neighborhood. In contrast, the devastation that results from personal disasters, such as fatal accidents, terminal diseases, or debilitating illnesses, is primarily limited to the immediate family. A common need among people experiencing disasters, of whatever kind, is to tell their stories. Yet there is typically a much greater comfort level in listening to personal stories about a community disaster than listening to a person's story about a tragic death of a family member.

Following the tornado, St. Peterites were given numerous opportunities to tell their stories, and the more details the better. Questions commonly asked included "Where were you during the tornado? How much damage did you have? What did the tornado look like? Sound like? Feel like?" By inviting everyone to tell their stories over and over again, these questions were the ultimate conversation icebreakers! Instant connections were made. The bonding that occurred among community members as they supported each other in the aftermath of the storm of storms was heartwarming.

Now, years after the tornado, there continue to be questions about the experience itself, the extensive damage, and the time involved in rebuilding efforts. As a friend observed, "Anytime someone brings up the tornado experience in a conversation, even fifty years from now, they will be able to tell their tornado story."

The devastation from the tornado was unreal, mind-boggling. But much more mind-boggling, from my perspective, was the devastation that occurs when a personal tornado rips apart the inner selves of many bereaved parents. This, too, resembles a war zone.

While I was able to talk about the general facts surrounding the accident that killed Erik and David multiple times, there were typically few follow-up questions about the death event, how it damaged our lives, or our rebuilding efforts. Others could not make themselves hear the specific details surrounding my sons' deaths or my husband's and my respective grief journeys. A bereaved parent was right on the mark when he said, "Almost everyone but grievers are so uncomfortable with the thought that their child could possibly die that they not only don't want to know or talk about it, they *actively* want not to know or talk about it."

Yet, in order to work through the event, to try to make some sense of it, a bereavement professional stated that every story of extreme loss needs to be told a minimum of fifty times. It was against this backdrop that I was struck by the countless number of times—many more than fifty times—that I was able to tell my tornado story because people *actively* wanted to know and talk about it.

What accounts for the difference in the levels of curiosity and ongoing interest expressed for a community disaster that directly impacts thousands of people versus a family tragedy in which the personal impact is much more limited in scope? What makes it more difficult to hear grief stories that relate to the death of a loved one, particularly a child or young adult child?

Is it possible that people are more comfortable continuing a conversation about the tornado because it is a fairly safe bet that they will also hear about all the significant improvements—newly built churches, community center, library and student union, a restored courthouse and a rebuilt tennis facility on a spiffed-up college campus, and extensive utility improvements—that have resulted in our community looking better than ever.

In this situation, it was possible to breathe easy and think, "Ah yes, all's well that ends well." But that adage doesn't work as well for the parents of the six-year-old boy who was killed in the tornado. Without any possibility of their situation ending well, all is not well in their lives, and perhaps that makes it a much harder story to *actively* want to know about.

Or does rephrasing the adage "What you don't know won't hurt you" to "What you don't think about won't happen" reflect an assumption that a tragic death can somehow be magically postponed or avoided if we don't think or talk about it?

To what extent does seeing obituaries day after day, or reading or hearing stories about death in all media forms, desensitize the public to death, grief, and pain? When death is seen primarily, as the song goes, "from a distance," it just doesn't seem that significant. Given the lack of awareness that grief may have no ending point, the need to talk about one's efforts at integrating grief into the fabric of life in a meaningful way often goes unrecognized.

Perhaps there is a fear that saying a deceased child's name would dredge up painful memories and add to the sadness. But it is impossible to be reminded of what has never been forgotten. Nor does talking about a child result in increased sadness when the heaviness of heart is always there. To the contrary, having one's child and one's grief acknowledged is usually appreciated.

This acknowledgment is best reflected in the permission to mourn. With this supportive gift there is:

- a safe place to give voice to one's grief experience;
- the freedom to discover how each grief journey is unique yet shares many similarities with others;
- encouragement to explore issues of spirituality important in the pursuit for meaning;
- understanding that readjusting one's life following the death of a child has no time limit; and
- the comfort of having one's new self accepted and valued.

Best of all, these suggestions are appropriate regardless of whether it has been weeks, months, or years since the child has died. They do not become outdated. Given that, support has its limits. It is not a magic wand that, when waved, will chase the pain away once and for all. While those who care about the bereaved want with all their hearts to say or do something that will lessen the grief, the level of sadness is unlikely to change in any significant way as a result of what anyone says or does.

If support does not diminish the level of sadness, then what is its purpose? The great and enduring gift of support is the warmth and comfort it brings to heavy and hurting hearts. When the bereaved are given permission to grieve their own way, support becomes grace-filled. Appropriate support also provides a much-needed lifeline to the future, empowering the bereaved to summon up the needed energy, courage, strength, and hope to integrate the reality of the death of their son or daughter into their lives.

I KNOW YOU ARE LISTENING TO ME WHEN

You come quietly into my private world and let me be.

*You really try to understand me
even when I am not making sense.*

*You grasp my point
even when it is against your sincere convictions.*

*You realize that the hour I took from you
has left you a bit tired and drained.*

*You allow me the dignity of making my own decisions
even though you think they might be wrong.*

*You do not take my problem from me
but allow me to deal with it in my own way.*

You hold back from giving me a word of "good advice."

*You do not offer me religious solace
when you sense I am not ready for it.*

*You give me enough room to discover for myself
what is really going on.*

*You accept my gift of gratitude
by telling me how being helpful makes you feel good.*

GLEN CRAWFORD
COMPASSIONATE FRIENDS NEWSLETTER
FAIRMONT CHAPTER, FAIRMONT, MN

WORDS FOR THE HOLIDAYS AND "ANY TIME"

"Happy Holidays!" Prior to the deaths of my sons, I had never realized how many holidays have the words "happy" or "merry" attached to the day or season. Very early on in my grief journey, I became acutely aware that those words frequently have a hollow ring for many bereaved during the holidays. As a result, I no longer assume that holidays and special events, such as birthdays, anniversaries, Mother's and Father's Day, are always happy.

While being confronted with the happy's and merry's can present a challenge at any time for grievers, it becomes much more challenging during the holidays when families traditionally gather together— Thanksgiving, Christmas, and New Year's. But, to be fair, the bereaved may sometimes convey the impression that all is well and back to normal again.

As an example, several Christmases after my sons' deaths, we were spending the holiday alone. But true to form, my husband put up the outside decorations shortly after Thanksgiving, and everything looked just as it had every Christmas prior to their deaths. Well, not exactly. Not having the emotional energy or motivation to go through the motions of decorating the living areas, I suggested that the inside decorating be limited to setting up the tree. And so, just before Christmas, my husband set up the tree—but without any lights or decorations. The saying "You can't judge a book by its cover" expresses the reality that what is seen on the outside may not resemble what is actually happening on the inside, whether it be the outside or inside of a house or the outside or inside of a soul.

Another subtle yet poignant acknowledgment that the holiday season may be difficult is reflected in the day of remembrance chosen for the Worldwide Candle Lighting Memorial—the second Sunday in December. In addition to commemorating the lives of all children who have died too soon, the day gently acknowledges that many bereaved families continue to mourn without a break during the holiday season and, in truth, all seasons. Another purpose of this day of remembrance, then, is to educate the public that the spirit of the season may be less than fully spirited for both new and seasoned grievers.

I have found New Year's to be a particularly difficult holiday. As the first new year following Erik and David's deaths approached, the hard fact that I would never be able to share any part of any new year with them again heightened the stark reality of their absence. In the year of their deaths, we had at least occupied the same world together for part of the year. And as I have entered each subsequent new year, I have been aware that as I am moving on in time, I am also moving farther and farther away from when they were a part of this world. Consequently, with each passing year the empty black hole where all the "what would've been" questions about their lives (marriage, children, jobs, etc.) have been dumped has become larger. In one of those "aha" moments, I realized how my feelings of emptiness were directly connected with my heaviness of heart. How paradoxical that something empty could feel heavy. Not surprisingly, a prime time for the emptiness to become heavier is during the holiday season.

Appropriate support would certainly go a long way in traversing the maze of the holiday daze. Many bereaved parents would welcome the opportunity to share their feelings about the holidays, regardless of the length of time since the death event. If someone would ask me, "The holidays are coming around again—how's it going for you this year?" or "How do the happy's and merry's sound to you this holiday season?", I would have the opportunity to be honest about where

I am in my grief journey. Rather than a breezy "Merry Christmas" or "Happy New Year," I would find it much more comforting if someone would say, "I'll be thinking of you this holiday season, knowing how much you'll be missing Erik and David." This sensitive greeting, in not presuming happiness, would openly acknowledge that grief, rather than taking a back seat, continues to shape what is meaningful and comforting during those weeks.

Sometimes a caring gesture communicates this message more powerfully than words ever could. One of my rituals has been placing luminaries (candles in brown bags) out by Erik and David's graves on their birthdays, their death date, Christmas, and Valentine's Day. After several years of some rather wimpy winters, we were having a real Minnesota winter once again—lots of snow and below-zero days. Knowing I needed to shovel a path to their site, I headed out to the cemetery Christmas Eve morning with a heavy heart. This was definitely not a task I, as a parent, had ever expected to be doing on Christmas. As I drove up to the site, I saw that a path had already been shoveled and the markers had been cleared off. Someone had not only remembered but, with that gesture, had given me permission to mourn. When I got home, I called to confirm my hunch that a special couple had given me this gift. I couldn't speak—except to say thanks—the emotion was overwhelming—but they knew. There was no need to explain why this act of kindness was so extraordinarily meaningful to me. Christmas was equally tough for them; more than six years earlier, their daughter had also been killed in an accident.

Acknowledging that it is not possible to cancel the holidays or go into hibernation for a couple of months, a bereaved sibling observed that holidays may feel more of a "responsibility" than a celebration (Heavilin & Heavilin, 2000). When that is the reality, some holiday traditions may continue as a way of acknowledging this responsibility while others may be modified in small or significant ways. Other rituals may be ignored completely, such as decorating the tree, when there is no compelling reason to expend any more energy from one's already depleted emotional reserves. Another option may be retreating to a different environment as a way of avoiding the hustle and bustle of the season.

Many bereaved parents have found unique and meaningful ways of including their child in family gatherings. One parent buys an angel each Christmas to symbolize how her daughter continues to be part of the family and to acknowledge the number of years that have gone by since her death. After cross-stitching Christmas stockings for my surviving son and his family, I cross-stitched stockings for Erik and David, which are placed by the tree during the holiday season. For families larger than ours, family members could place a written memory in a stocking or memory basket that could be read as part of the gift opening or during a meal. In that way the younger ones, who may never have known this family member, could get a sense of their personality, how much they are loved, and how they continue to be a member of the family.

Looking for a holiday card that fits one's changed life may also be somewhat challenging. But there are options! One option is to forgo sending cards completely; another option is to make a computer-generated card. In this day and age anyone, of any age, can make his or her own cards! Purely by happenstance, my preschool-age grandsons painted "something" that was abstract yet very pleasing to the eye. The gentle blues, warm pinkish-reds, and subtle yellow-greens symbolized, for me, what the spirit world might be like—warm, colorful, peaceful. Their paintings were scanned into the computer and out came two nontraditional-looking cards. While they did not look at all "Christmasy," they were perfect for our holiday message: "May Peace Be Your Gift This Christmas and Your Treasure in the New Year." And so began a meaningful tradition of sending out cards that reflected our grandchildren's progression in their artistic development over the years.

Yet another option is available from support groups or magazines, such as the Sudden Infant Death Center and *Bereavement* magazine. Being acutely aware of the need for alternative holiday cards, these organizations provide a wonderful service by offering cards that focus on the themes of peace, hope, and love.

I have read, and believe, that the kindest wish that can be extended to any bereaved person is a wish for a measure of comfort or peace. When experienced, in whatever form that is meaningful, feeling comforted has passed the test of time for being one of the most effective ways of warming the heart.

A primary characteristic of hope is that, far from being static, it changes its form as situations change. When the hope that one's child will experience all of life's stages and milestones has been lost, hope, of necessity, changes dramatically. Following a child's death, hope provides the spark plug that helps generate the energy or the "oomph" to carry the bereaved through each lap of their grief journey.

For anyone to be the best they can be, healthy doses of love are needed even under the most ordinary of circumstances. As the most lasting renewable energy source on this planet, nothing could be more important to one's well-being when circumstances become extraordinary.

May comfort, hope, and love be the gifts given and received during each holiday season and a treasure for any time.

In times of darkness,
Love sees...

In times of silence,
Love hears...

In times of doubt,
Love hopes...

In times of sorrow,
Love comforts...

And, in all times,
Love remembers.

FROM A HALLMARK CARD

SPOUSES AND SURVIVING SIBLINGS

The death of a child can change the dynamics of family relationships as nothing else can. Since parents and siblings typically live (or have lived) in the same household, they are not only grieving the death of their child or sibling, they are also confronted with having to readjust to different relationships with each other. Following the accidental deaths of his two teen-age brothers, the one surviving sibling said, "It's going to be awfully quiet around here." That sense of "quiet" will take on many different dimensions for spouses and surviving siblings.

Spouses: Several months after my sons' deaths, a widow told me how lucky I was to have a spouse. She reflected how my husband and I could support each other in our grief, whereas a bereaved spouse must grieve alone.

Contrary to prevailing assumptions, spouses in the throes of a grief beyond belief tend to have a more difficult time supporting each other following the death of a child than with other life losses. To illustrate, when an elderly parent dies, the adult child is generally the primary griever. In this situation, the spouse of the adult child likely has the emotional capacity to provide support. But this is not the case when parents are confronted with their worst nightmare—the death of their child.

The old adage "Blood is thicker than water" describes the loyalty of family members to each other. When it comes to the parent-child relationship, the blood connection with a child is likely stronger than in any other relationship. Parents have typically devoted, and perhaps sacrificed, a significant amount of their available emotional, mental, and financial resources to raising, nurturing, and loving their child. Then their child dies! Nothing will ever be the same for either spouse. Both of their lives have been turned inside out and upside down at the same time but not in exactly the same way. Even though the lenses used to look at life post-loss are completely different from their pre-loss lenses, their individual personalities and unique needs result in each spouse wearing his or her own unique lenses.

While the grief responses of bereaved parent couples tend to be somewhat similar in the first weeks, perhaps months, following the death of their child, their mourning paths will likely diverge over time. One spouse may prefer talking about his or her grief endlessly, while the other may prefer to reflect on grief alone. Activities that provide meaning or purpose in life may vary significantly between spouses. The frequency of grave site visits or how the child is remembered may also become a bone of contention. The number of issues that can conceivably increase marital tensions following the death of a child is mind boggling. Is it any wonder that spousal reactions may be diametrically opposed to each other? Is it any wonder that spouses may have a difficult time supporting each other?

The mutual vulnerability of each spouse makes it unlikely that they would have the capacity to consistently provide each other with emotional support. When emotions are so intense, fragile, and changeable, and without any predictability or pattern to mourning, either spouse can "fall apart" without any warning. The waves of grief can be triggered by a multitude of sensory cues, such as hearing a song or story, watching a game, catching a whiff of their child's shaving lotion or favorite perfume, eating certain foods or driving by a familiar landmark. Acknowledging this reality would help lessen the possibility of feeling shortchanged when the emotional support of either spouse falls short of what is needed.

I learned rather quickly that my husband and I were each on uniquely separate and solitary journeys. Even though we were grieving the deaths of the same children, our grief work could not be shared. Teamwork would not work in this instance. Just as I could not feel his pain or sadness, he was not able to feel my pain and sadness. We would need to grieve "alone together"—an oxymoron, to be sure.

As an introvert and not feeling as connected with the world of my old self, I was uncomfortable being in certain situations, whereas my husband, as somewhat of an extrovert, appeared to adapt with less difficulty. It took awhile before we realized that grieving in a particular way was neither right nor wrong, good nor bad, but just different. Just as important was a mutual respect of those differences.

Even though the myth that the divorce rate for bereaved parents is as high as 70 percent has basically been dispelled, a child's death inevitably places additional stresses on a marriage. Many factors, including the relationship pre-loss, the cause of death, age of a child, and circumstances surrounding the death, influence the marriage post-loss. Additionally, the ongoing responsibilities of family, job, or community likely drain more energy from the bereaved couple's emotional reserves than was the case prior to their child's death. There may be countless times when they feel as if they've run a mental and emotional marathon on an empty tank. Given all that, it is inevitable that the impact of a child's death on a marriage would be felt over time—for better or for worse—as the vows say.

Understanding and affirming a couple's individual similarities and differences can alleviate some of the tensions of different grieving preferences and permit more energy to be directed toward readjusting their individual lives and their shared lives over time.

Surviving Siblings: A common theme expressed by many bereaved siblings is that they feel forgotten. They tell of all the times people ask them, "How are your parents' doing?" when they long for someone to ask them, "How are YOU doing?" They tell of how conversations are concluded with a "Now you take care of your parents," when they could use a few shoulders to lean on themselves. It is not surprising, under these circumstances, that bereaved siblings often feel left out of the grieving loop.

When the surviving sibling is married, they may perceive themselves as being the last link of the grieving chain and all but forgotten. Often the grief of the surviving spouse, children and parents is considered to be more intense than that of bereaved siblings, when in fact the grief and pain has a unique impact on each family member's life. To recognize that grief involves the entire family, joining all the links of the chain together to make a circle would be a start in correcting the assumption that grieving is somehow hierarchal.

Another reality is that parents, consumed with their own grief, likely find it difficult to attend to their surviving children's needs. When there is no one available to fill the gap, bereaved siblings may feel as if they have been left high and dry to fend for themselves and forgotten once again.

Young adult children, having left the parental home, possibly live in other parts of the country. This potentially leaves them without an adequate support system, which would have been accessible to them in their home community. Conversely, siblings living in a distant or urban community may find it easier to separate themselves from their grief. When they are not confronted with visible reminders of the loss each day, it may seem as if it were not quite as real; that is, something that is out of sight is easier to put out of mind. As a coping mechanism, some go underground with their grief, where it smolders until some other life event causes it to resurface or manifest itself in some form.

The death of a sibling may well be the first close, personal encounter surviving siblings have had with death. Death is no longer something that happens to someone else or to the elders in their family. It can happen to someone in their own age group. It can happen in their own family—and more significantly, it not only *can* happen, it *did* happen! They have learned at an earlier age than most that there is no guarantee that one will not experience a significant or catastrophic loss in life. They have learned that life is not fair; that the rain falls on the just and unjust alike; and that some very bad things happen to some very good people. Besides the world of the parents, the world of the surviving brothers or sisters may also have been shattered.

So that they know that they have not been forgotten, siblings need to have their grief sensitively acknowledged and lovingly supported as they also do the hard work of integrating the impact and finality of their brother or sister's death into their lives.

A DEATH HAS OCCURRED

A death has occurred and everything is changed by this event.
We are painfully aware that life can never be the same again,
that yesterday is over,
that relationships once rich have ended.

But there is another way to look upon this truth.
If life went on the same without the presence of the one who has died,
we could only conclude that the life we remember
made no contribution, filled no space, meant nothing.

The fact that the person left behind a place
that cannot be filled is a high tribute to this individual.
Life can be the same after a trinket has been lost,
but never after the loss of a treasure.

PAUL IRION

THE QUEST
TO KNOW

The beliefs that had formed my foundation for living from childhood into middle adulthood were put to the ultimate test following the deaths of Erik and David. What had seemed so reasonable and had given my life order and predictability no longer provided the solid underpinnings on which I could center or ground my life. In their place were questions, many questions related to life and death and life after death, which haunted me. Believing was no longer enough. I needed "to know" as much as possible about these rather daunting issues.

A concrete example of the need "to know" occurred following the tornado that ripped through our community. Immediately after the tornado, countless numbers of people tried to reach family or friends by phone to find out, first and foremost, if they were safe and, secondly, if they still had a home. Within a relatively short period of time, the proverbial grapevine (or mediavine) had provided enough information to reassure most people that those they were wondering about were probably safe. And for some, this amount of information was enough. For others, it was not enough to hear about what others knew or thought they knew about the people in question. They needed "to know"! And so they came to St. Peter. They had to see and hear for themselves how their friends or family members were really doing. They came so they could know with 100 percent certainty that those they loved or cared about were safe.

Once phone lines were restored, my husband and I became more aware of the persistent efforts friends had made to verify our safety and well-being. They continued calling us until they reached us—they needed to hear our voices tell the story; secondhand information was not good enough. They needed "to know."

And so, would it be so unusual for moms and dads to want "to know" what had happened to their children following their deaths? It would seem to be a very "Mom and Dad" thing to do. What is believed about death and/or life after death may be enough for many bereaved parents, but for others, beliefs may not be enough. My heart has persisted in trying to find a reason for my sons' deaths, even though my head knows that no reason given could ever justify that event. My heart has continued to search for clues that would give me the concrete and certain answers about life after death when my head knows there is no human way to figure it all out. In spite of this, I have been driven to do what I can to close the gap between my heart and my head.

Because of this need "to know," much time has been spent exploring such issues as after-death communication, predestination, the influence God has on life in general or individual lives in particular, along with other life and death issues.

After-Death Communication: Believing in an afterlife gave rise to a host of other questions about the what, whys, and wheres of the spirit world—Where is it? What's it like? Where are my sons? And, more to the point, if my sons continue to exist, what, if anything, do they know about what has gone on in this world? Are their spirits keeping their eyes on me? Have they shared special occasions with me? I talk to them all the time. Have they heard me? Have I missed obvious signs of their communication? Do they know how much I love them? Miss them? How they continue to be a part of my life? A part of my family? The questions have been endless.

I have yearned to communicate with my sons, in whatever form possible, just one more time. Many would say I'm asking for the impossible, and perhaps I am. Yet many people have dreams that are subsequently interpreted as being messages from their loved ones in the spirit world. Since I rarely recall any dreams, communicating with my sons in this way seems highly unlikely. All the same, I've had several "sixth-sense" type experiences that have given me reason to consider the possibility that I may have been in the company of my sons' supportive presence and guidance.

The first experience occurred at a memorial service at the high school where David had been a math teacher and tennis coach. As part of the service, the crowd, led by the girls' tennis team sang, or rather tried to sing, the school's fight song. It was sung very sorrowfully and with no fight whatsoever. Then I "heard" what I interpreted as David saying to me, "Mom, they're doing a terrible job. They're not doing their best at all; they've got to do better." So after they were through, I yelled out to the crowd of more than a thousand as loud as I could, surprising everyone but probably most of all myself, "David would say you can do better than that; let's sing it again and louder this time." And so they did. The performance, however, was still lackluster. Again, David's voice inside my head instructed me, "They're still not doing their best, Mom—one more time." And so obedient Mom yelled out again, "It's still not your best. One more time—you can do it." And while it was still not their best by far, it was better. Was I really being David's voice? Was he really giving me those instructions? Or was it just a very bereaved mom knowing what he would have done? While it was completely and totally uncharacteristic of anything I would ever do, it was not unlike David at all. It would have been exactly what he would have done.

Another interesting experience occurred about eighteen months after the accident. After waking up from a nap, I had this overpowering sensation that there was someone else in the room. (I was home alone.) A split second later I thought, "Is it—could it be— Erik and David?" Skeptic that I am, I thought I was losing my mind. But the presence continued. I felt as if I were wrapped up in and completely surrounded by a wonderful sensation of peace. I remember thinking that if this was what peace really felt like, the feeling was certainly not part of this world. It was wonderful! At the same time, I continued my internal questioning. Had I had been dreaming? Was my imagination working overtime? Had I truly experienced the presence of my sons? I wanted to think so but, again, I didn't know *for sure*. I do know that I have experienced nothing like it before, nor have I since, but if it happened again, I would forgo any questioning and just absorb and treasure the moment. And if it was my sanity going, so be it!

Since then I have read several books on angels and after-death communication. Compelling stories illustrate the various types of spirit visitations that people have experienced. Paranormal experiences include the sense of a strong presence, visits through dreams, seeing a loved one in a vision, an overwhelming odor associated with the deceased, being touched by them, or noticing that items have mysteriously moved.

Bereaved parents frequently tell of having paranormal experiences that were subsequently taken as signs that their children have communicated with them. Having the hope that there is the possibility of a real time connection between the spirit world and this world has provided many with a measure of comfort. The interest in learning more about this topic is validated by sessions that are routinely filled to capacity at the National Compassionate Friends Conferences. Interestingly, even though the prospect of life after death is the major underpinning of most religious denominations, the possibility of communicating with loved ones on the "other side" does not have what could be called "mainstream acceptance."

One final experience: I was one of the speakers at the dedication of the David and Erik Aasen classroom in a tennis facility at our local college. I am, to say the least, a reluctant public speaker, but I wanted to say something that reflected their philosophy that skills learned through sports participation are transferrable to a multitude of life situations. Prior to the dedication, I went out to my sons' graves and said, "Okay, guys, what do you think of this?" and read my speech. As I finished, I was surprised at how confident I felt. It was as if they were saying to me, "You've got it right, Mom." Then I asked them to help me get through the speech without falling apart.

Prior to presenting I was more than a little nervous. But once I started speaking, I thought, "What's going on here?" It was as if the voices of Erik and David were behind my voice and I had been, more or less, put on autopilot. My voice—or was it their voices?—sounded very assured and confident. Were they actually helping me? Were they really there? Unbelievably (or naively), I was so convinced they were the mystical energy behind my voice that I decided that I would put this feeling to the test and just stop talking when I came to the last paragraph and let them carry on. In a flash I became wordless. In the next second, when I began speaking again, I was on my own. The mysterious energy had left my voice, and I stumbled through the remaining paragraph of my speech. At that point I was 98 percent convinced that Erik and David's spirits had given me the assist I had asked for when giving my speech.

On hearing about these experiences, there are some who would say, "Of course you were experiencing your sons' presence. It's as plain as the nose on your face." Others would be just as convinced that these incidents were merely a product of a vivid imagination or wishful thinking. And what did I think? I was, as usual, in the middle. I wanted to believe, with every fiber of my being, that my sons' presence had been with me, but I didn't know *for sure*. And while there is the hope and perhaps the belief, the quest has remained the same—to know, to be sure.

One of David's friends is convinced that David has visited him, talked to him, and hugged him during a dream and while in a waking state. He has no doubts. There has been no skepticism. Nothing anyone could say would shake his conviction. In being so completely open and receptive to having a sixth-sense experience, is it possible that this friend is more likely to sense David's spirit trying to connect with him than someone like me, who is not completely convinced? What I have craved to know with absolute certainty is still only a possibility, but that is definitely an improvement over no possibility.

Predestination: Another issue that bereaved parents have had to reconcile within themselves is that of the interminable "if only's." "If only" I had set my alarm clock, we would have left for Chicago an hour earlier on that fateful Thanksgiving Day. After waking late, "if only" I hadn't pushed Erik and David to hurry up, we would have been on that part of the road minutes later. In every scenario of the "if only's" that I've played over and over in my head, we were no longer in the wrong place at the wrong time. But then came the next question: What if this was part of a plan? Then questions surrounding predestination came to the forefront. Then all of the "if only's" would not have made a difference. Everything that happened on that morning was predestined to happen.

Was there a predestined time for my sons' deaths? Was there a clock ticking away that knew the time of their demise? The predestination question began to seem more plausible when I heard the following stories.

A friend related that in his last conversation with David the night before the accident, they were discussing, among other things, life insurance. This friend, who sold life insurance, questioned David about his decision to buy several policies when he was still single. David replied that he was protecting his future, and if something happened to him, he would be leaving a "nice gift for my parents." (The funds established several scholarships in my sons' honor and memory.)

During the same evening, Erik, a physical therapy student, was dictating his clinical notes for the last day of a clinical rotation. The staff said he routinely ended his dictation with a humorous remark. However, his last comment on this particular tape was "And this is my last tape forever and ever. Alleluia." It was probably meant to be humorous, but instead it was ominously prophetic. What would possess him to say such a thing? Did they both have some kind of premonition that their lives may be ending? With a maturity level seemingly beyond their years and an apparent awareness of the fragility of life, were they, in a sense, "ready" to die?

In reading the literature and conducting research on post-death communication, Kay Woods (1998) concluded that there seem to be indications that a person's soul knows, even though their conscious self does not, that he or she is about to die. These instances seem to be associated most frequently with a sudden death. To illustrate, family members or friends often recall specific words or actions that did not seem completely out of place at the time but post-death seem to be a "sign" that the soul knew that death was near. At other times, finding an item such as a poem, song, or artwork among their son's or daughter's personal possessions is also taken as a "sign" by parents that their child's soul was saying goodbye. Were my sons' souls saying goodbye?

We learned about this next incident more than a year after the accident. During a visit, David's friend Sarah tentatively asked us, "Do you believe in predestination?" I replied, "At this point, I have no idea what I believe—I'm open to anything." She then shared with us a telephone conversation she'd had with a friend about three months before the accident. This friend had asked Sarah if she was okay; the answer was "I'm fine." He then asked her if she had been in an accident; the answer was "No." Next question: "Do you know if Aaron is okay?" Answer: "As far as I know he's okay." (A later call verified this.) After the accident this friend called Sarah again and told her more of what had prompted the original call several months before. This friend had dreamed of a car accident involving fatalities, and Sarah's name had been emblazoned across the accident scene along with the two letters AA. These letters were now obviously interpreted to mean Aasen.

Were these signs that this tragedy was going to happen and that there was no stopping it? How many people have looked back and thought, "Did I miss the signs? Did I miss my chance to intervene?" Gnawing, nagging questions. While I was still unsure what I thought, much less believed, about predestination, it certainly seemed more plausible than it once had. For others, the possibility that their child's death was predestined as part of a plan gives some meaning to the event—there was a reason, unknown to the parents or loved ones, for the death to happen when it did.

Why, God Why?! I have listened to prayers a lot more carefully than I did prior to the deaths of my sons. Now, whenever I hear a prayer for a safe journey I think, "Not necessarily so." There have been a countless number of times when being in the wrong place at the wrong time resulted in a tragedy and praying did not change the outcome.

In spite of fervent prayers for a safe journey, did God say "Time's up" for a certain number of children because their parents were strong enough to handle adversity? And what about natural disasters, such as floods or tornados, that destroyed some homes on a block but left others virtually untouched? Does this mean that God spares certain families whose good works have made a difference? Does God destroy the homes of those who have fallen by the wayside or have not made the best use of their God-given talents, and therefore, deserve to be taught a lesson? Is a specific child's death part of a detailed plan, or does a higher power direct the overall design but from that point on people are, more or less, faceless to God and left to fend for themselves?

Questions, questions, questions! What are the answers? Why do people, good people, experience senseless tragedies? Harold Kushner's book, *When Bad Things Happen To Good People* (1981), sheds a different light on why things may happen, which differs from the predestination or "their faith can handle it" perspective. In studying and reflecting on the book of Job, Rabbi Kushner concluded that God is not totally powerful and cannot overrule the laws established during the creation process.

With this view, God neither allows nor causes tragedies. Instead, they are caused by bad luck, bad people, random occurrences, or by the inflexible and precise laws of nature that results in, for example, the predictable effects of gravity and being able to pinpoint exactly when the sun will rise and set each day. These reliable natural laws treat good and bad people alike, regardless of race, color, or creed. Simply put, tragedies are the result of random occurrences or acts of nature as opposed to acts of God. With this view, God cannot be blamed for all the bad things that happen to good people. The flip side is that any near misses or close calls, where lives have been spared, are probably related to these same natural laws along with some good luck, good people, and random occurrences.

It is likely that almost everyone will have, at minimum, a small-scale Job-like experience sometime in their lives. So like Job, I could cry out, "Why, God, why?" I could vent my anger and frustration at God for the injustice and unfairness of the world. I could tell God off, so to speak, and give this higher being a piece of my mind. And, if God is not totally powerful, then this higher being would theoretically understand and be just as angry and appalled at all the tragedies, injustices, and oppression that occur in the world and grieve alongside the bereaved.

Kushner asserts that if God were not perceived as the cause of what happens in our everyday lives, good and bad, fair and unfair, prayers would no longer be focused on a laundry list of wishes and wants. Instead, prayers would be more appropriately directed toward the capacity to love unconditionally and forgive, to be more compassionate or sensitive to the needs of others, to have the courage to advocate for justice or fairness for the oppressed and mistreated in our society, and the strength and hope to manage and survive life's tragedies and adversities. That would appear to be about all we could pray for. But then, maybe, that would be quite a bit.

It has been rather difficult to mentally juxtapose Kushner's theory of why bad things happen to good people with the predestination possibility. And even though I'm still searching for the "for sure" answers to these puzzling questions—even though these questions have remained shrouded in mystery—it certainly has not meant that my quest to know could not continue. By continuing the process of searching, there has been the hope that I would come upon some nugget of information or insight about life and death, and life after death, which, perhaps, would bring some additional meaning to the quest to know as I continue my grief journey.

PARABLE OF THE TWINS

Once upon a time, twin boys were conceived in the same womb.
Weeks passed, and the twins developed.
As their awareness grew, they laughed with joy:
"Isn't it great that we were conceived?
Isn't it great to be alive?"

Together, the twins explored their world.
When they found their mother's cord that gave them life,
they sang with joy: "How great is our mother's love,
that she shares her own life with us!"

As weeks stretched into months,
the twins noticed how much each was changing.
"What does it mean?" asked one. "It means that our stay in this world
is drawing to an end," said the other. "But I don't want to go!
I want to stay in here always," said one. "We have no choice
but maybe there is life after birth!" said the other.
"But how can there be?" responded one. "We will shed our life cord,
and how is life possible without it? Besides, we have seen evidence
that others were here before us and none of them have returned
to tell us that there is life after birth. No, this is the end."

And so one fell into deep despair, saying: "If conception ends in birth,
what is the purpose of life in the womb? It is meaningless!
Maybe there is no mother after all?"

"But there has to be," protested the other. "How else did we get here?
How do we remain alive?"

"Have you ever seen our mother?" said the one.
"Maybe she lives only in our minds. Maybe we made her up,
because the ideas made us feel good?"

And so the last days in the womb were filled with deep questioning
and fear. Finally, the moment of birth arrived.

When the twins had passed from their world, they opened their eyes.
They cried. For what they saw exceeded their fondest dreams.

AUTHOR UNKNOWN

FAITH
COMMUNITIES

As part of their mission, churches, synagogues, and temples provide much-needed support for the bereaved immediately after the death of a loved one and, perhaps, for a few months following the loss. While short-term support may be sufficient for the majority of losses by death, it is not adequate for those losses having an extremely high intensity level. Yet the traditions and beliefs of faith communities have reinforced the norm that mourning should be short-term.

With many memorial services focusing on celebrating the life of the deceased regardless of the age at which he or she died, the implication is that the funeral provides the transition point between mourning and celebration. There are certainly many situations in which the celebration of life is the appropriate mantra. For those who experienced a debilitating illness in their elder years and/or suffered a decline in their ability to function mentally, death may be perceived as a welcome release from their physical bodies. At those times, it is appropriate to celebrate the life they lived. For others, who died after living a long life, having experienced each of life's developmental stages and having had at least the opportunity to fulfill their dreams, it is also appropriate to celebrate their legacy.

While their children's short time in this world was something to be very thankful for, how much more thankful bereaved parents would be if their sons and daughters could have lived out their lives in their own unique ways; if they could have lived out the promise of their future. When lives are so cruelly cut short, celebrating these lives without affirming and validating the stark reality that there was so much living left to do minimizes, in a sense, the tragedy of premature death. With scant acknowledgment that the natural order of death has been subverted, bereaved parents may feel as if their right to mourn has been taken away from them.

There also may be an assumption that having a firm belief in a specific religion's particular tenets, especially the promise that the deceased is safe with God in a better place, is all that is needed to decrease the grief intensity and bring closure to the grieving process. No more questions need to be asked, no more doubts need to be raised.

Even though I've never had a second's worry that heaven's gates did not open wide for Erik and David, believing in an after life of some sort has not lessened my grief. The assumption that it does (or should) misses the point completely. Rather, the primary issue has been that my sons are no longer occupying their space in *this* world—no longer here to touch, to see, to talk with, to interact with. That's what's been at the core of my grief. Written on cold black stone, their time on earth is marked by a much-too-short dash separating their birth date and death date. This too-short dash is also at the core of my grief.

In contrast, the social and theological climate surrounding death and grief issues could be markedly improved if the words of Dietrich Bonhoeffer were taken to heart. Bonhoeffer, whose theological writings have been widely respected for a number of decades, had it right when he wrote *"Nothing can make up for the absence of someone whom we love and it would be wrong to try to find a substitute; we must simply hold out and see it through. That sounds very hard at first, but at the same time it is a great consolation, for the gap, as long as it remains unfilled, preserves the bonds between us. It is nonsense to say that God fills the gap; God doesn't fill it, but on the contrary, keeps it empty and so helps us keep alive our former communion with each other, even at the cost of pain."* With these words Bonhoeffer acknowledges fully that a feeling of emptiness is to be expected following a high-intensity loss and is, at the same time, a sign that the connection with a loved one cannot and should not be broken.

Faith communities have a moral obligation to lead the way in being a community of ongoing support and love for those who continue to grieve and hurt years after the death of their loved one. Part of their leadership role should include educating their congregation on how to be more supportive to bereaved members. By acknowledging the reality that lifelong grief is a potential consequence of a catastrophic loss, faith communities could be a primary impetus behind a much-needed correction in how our culture views grief and would, in turn, become a safer place for the bereaved to come for solace and support.

HOW DO YOU LIVE YOUR DASH

I read of a woman who stood to speak at the funeral of a friend.

*She referred to the dates that would be on her tombstone
from the beginning...to the end.*

*She noted that first came her date of birth
and then spoke the death date with tears. (1900–1970)*

*But she said what mattered most of all
was the dash between those years.*

*For the dash represents all the time
that she spent alive on earth*

*And now only those who loved her
know what that little line is worth.*

*For it matters not how much we own—
the cars...the house...the cash,*

*What matters most is how we live
and love and how we spend our dash.*

*So think about this long and hard:
Are there things you'd like to change?*

*For you never know how much time there is,
that can still be rearranged.*

*If we could just slow down enough to consider
what's true and real,*

*And always try to understand
the way other people feel.*

*And be less quick to criticize,
and show appreciation more*

*And love the people in our lives
like we've never loved before.*

*If we treat each other with respect,
and more often go the extra mile*

*Remembering that this special dash
might only last a little while.*

*So, when your eulogy's being read
with your life's actions to rehash...*

*Would you be proud of the things they say
about how you spent your dash?*

AUTHOR UNKNOWN

HAPPENINGS
AT THE GRAVE SITE

Going to the grave sites of loved ones meets varying needs—the need to remember, reflect, meditate, or grieve; the need to be at a place that is set apart, where it is possible to ponder the meaning of death, life, grief, and love, to cry out for answers to the unanswerable questions—those agonizing whys.

I used to think that nothing much happened during cemetery visits. Much to my surprise, there have been several meaningful experiences that have happened while visiting my sons' graves over the years.

Unexpected Support: On a beautiful summer Sunday, I went out to the cemetery to spend some time with Erik and David. It was one of those days when the grass is green and the sky is blue, and under normal circumstances, it would have been a great day to be alive.* It was about seven months after the accident. I was sitting on a blanket and the horror and finality of the tragedy was overwhelming me. When I thought the pain couldn't possibly get worse, *it got worse!* I was screaming and crying. I was out of control. If anything was beyond endurance, this was it. I was startled and surprised to hear a car door shut. I turned and looked, and walking toward me was my son's best friend from high school. I cannot imagine what he must have thought at seeing this wailing woman, but he was not deterred and kept on walking toward me. He stayed when it would have been

---

*David's signature quote was "The grass is green, the sky is blue—it's a great day to be alive." David greeted his class or tennis team with this quote every day, regardless of the weather. It reflected his philosophy that life was a gift to be lived to the fullest each and every day.

a lot easier to leave than to contend with me and my grief for an hour. I have frequently wondered how it was that he came out at that exact moment. I have imagined that my sons knew I needed support, knew I was totally losing it, did not want me to be alone, and "sent" a dear friend to be with me. Wishful thinking? Could be...but then again, maybe not.

Insight Gained: It was the first Memorial Day (1995) after the accident. My husband and I were sitting on the grass by our sons' graves (to say words like "graves" and "cemetery" in conjunction with "my sons" has continued, to this day, to be so unreal—so unbelievable). We saw a couple walking toward us—the parents of a young woman who had also been killed in a car accident, just twelve days before our sons. This young woman had been engaged at the time of her death. We exchanged condolences. I can't recall exactly how the topic came up, but I remember the young woman's mom saying that she had heard that her daughter's fiancé had started dating, and she was struggling with how to accept that reality. The discussion that followed incorporated these ideas. Prior to the deaths of my sons I was always shocked when I heard that someone had begun dating or had remarried shortly after the death of a spouse. I would think, "What kind of respect is that? If one's spouse dies, no big deal, just go shopping for a replacement model." After the deaths of my sons, I understood like I never could have before that the empty hole in one's life is so deep and wide that there is a tremendous, if not desperate, need to fill the void—to meet one's ever-present need for companionship and love. I also discovered something else. Finding a new partner does not mean that one has stopped loving or grieving the lost spouse or significant other. The "old love" continues even as a "new love" is incorporated into one's life.

On different occasions this young woman's mom has expressed appreciation for that unplanned conversation. Certainly none of us expected to become involved in a meaningful discussion on that grave site visit.

Encountering Humor: On Memorial Day, 1997, David's assistant tennis coach placed a bouquet of flowers by his marker. When I went out to water the flowers the first time, I noted how beautiful the flowers were and watered them. The second time out I thought, "These flowers are still looking great" (and watered them); third time, "These peonies are sure holding up well" (and watered them); fourth time, "These flowers are amazing," but chalked it up to the cool weather (and watered them). At the fifth visit, about two weeks after Memorial Day, the flowers still looked as if they had just been freshly cut. At this point I finally asked myself, "What IS it with these flowers, anyway?" and took the time to take a closer look. As I realized, "Oh my gosh, I've been watering fake flowers," I yelled out as loud as I could, **"OKAY YOU GUYS, YOU CAN STOP LAUGHING ANYTIME NOW."** I could literally see and hear them laughing hysterically and saying, "Duh, Mom, it's about time. It sure took you long enough. We were wondering when you were going to finally catch on." Was I surprised? You bet! How was it that I did not become suspicious of these flowers' longevity before? It may be a lame excuse, but since I usually watered the flowers before going to work, I needed to remain as detached from the reality of the situation as I possibly could in order to keep my composure.

The flowers went through three seasons—fall, summer, and winter—through smoldering summer heat and the bone-chilling cold of winter; through shattering thunderstorms and raging snowstorms. And who knows, they might still be there if a tornado hadn't come along on March 29, 1998. Tornadoes are notorious for not sparing anything in their paths, including cemeteries.

The Return of a Memory Container: My sons' grave sites are in a cemetery that is about as old as St. Peter itself. Over a period of about 150 years, the cemetery's 200 or more pine trees had grown so they towered over the landscape and provided a sense of majesty, dignity, and comfort to those who came to grieve and remember their loved ones. Following my sons' deaths, visitors to their grave sites began leaving mementos. As a means of protecting and sharing these gifts of love with others I placed clear plastic airtight canisters with Erik and David's pictures taped on the outside by their markers. As people came, these "memory containers" were filled with pictures, eagle feathers, flowers, tennis balls, Christmas ornaments, letters, ribbons, a ring, and a medal—many gifts of love. At the time of the tornado the two containers were stuffed full of memories and tributes.

As the tornado began its descent into St. Peter, the cemetery was one of the first places hit, and there was no mercy. Every one of those majestic trees on the hillside was mowed down. None remained—not even parts of the trunks. People seeing the devastation for the first time could not believe their eyes. It would be hard to imagine a more compelling "before and after" scene. The place looked ravaged, stark, barren, and desolate. Just as many find it difficult to talk about death and grief, the initial reaction of many who came to see the damage for themselves was to avert their eyes or turn away from the complete and total destruction that was staring them in the face. Obviously, the memory containers were nowhere to be found in all the mess. Who knows where they had landed; paper items had been found more than 150 miles away. And with many household items looking as if they had been pulverized, would the memory containers be recognizable if they were found?

So I bought a new memory container, taped my sons' pictures on it, and replicated some of the items that had been in the original canisters. Now, every time I drove out to the cemetery, my first priority was to assure myself that the canister was still there. On one day my eyes seemed to be seeing double—where there had been one canister, now there were two. I thought I must be seeing things. I got out of the car, walked toward their grave sites, and could hardly believe what I saw—

one of the original memory containers. It was in one piece, with nary a speck of tornado debris on the outside, and all the "stuff" was still inside. Where had it been found? How far had it "flown"? How could it possibly have survived? Who found it and cleaned it up? Who knew where it belonged? Who brought it back to its rightful place so that it was there on that day, Mother's Day, 1998?! I was overwhelmed with gratitude and grief.

A Possibility of Synchronicity: I have no regular pattern for grave site visitations. For my longer visits, I tend to choose nice weather days; spreading a quilt on their site, I sit for a couple of hours to write or reflect. More than six years into my grief journey I went, for the first time, early on a Saturday morning. Since my purpose in going was to spruce up their grave sites, I planned to be there for just a few minutes. As I was going about my task, I noticed a guy wandering from grave to grave on the hillside. Even though he was some distance away, he looked to be about Erik and David's age. As he continued to wander, I began to wonder if he was looking for their site. At the same time I noticed he was casting glances my way. As I was driving away, I came within a few feet of where he was standing and rolled down my window. Without a moment's hesitation, he looked directly at me and said, "Brian Meyer." Both of our hunches were confirmed. One of David's college friends, Brian had not been back to St. Peter since the funeral. Because of his numbness from that day, the time that had elapsed, and the tornado-changed landscape, he had been unable to remember the specific location of their graves until he saw me and put two and two together. Quickly I pulled out my quilt from the car and, settling down in Erik and David's space, we talked for two comforting hours. That we were in the same place at the same time (before 8:30 a.m.) seemed to go beyond coincidence. It felt as if it was meant to be. In believing that it was synchronicity that brought us together for this visit, we found an additional measure of meaning, imagining that

Erik and David's spirits had arranged this grave site happening and were now sharing it with us.

Even though the tears have flowed, many times copiously, these rather surprising and spontaneous happenings have resulted in unexpected blessings in my grief journey. For that I have been thankful!

In one sense there is no death.
The life of a soul on earth lasts beyond his (her) departure.

You will always feel that life touching yours,
that voice speaking to you, that spirit looking out of other eyes,
talking to you in the familiar things he (she) touched,
worked with, loved as familiar friends.

He (She) lives on in your life and in the lives
of all others that knew him (her).

ANGELO PATRI

"OUT OF THE BLUE" ANGELS

"Out of the blue"—an event that catches one totally off guard, an event that appears out of nowhere with no warning, just as if it had dropped out of the sky, "out of the blue." I have come to recognize the various twists to the "out of the blue" expression as I have thought about the accident that killed my sons.

On Thanksgiving Day, 1994, my husband and I, along with Erik and David, were continuing the relatively new tradition of going to Chicago to spend the holiday with our oldest son and his family. Because Erik wanted to come home early to play in a volleyball tournament, he and David were traveling in a separate car. Before we left Erik made the comment, "Got the survival kit, Mom," teasing me, because he knew I always wanted him to be prepared when traveling in winter weather. Laughing, I said, "We have nothing to worry about today, Erik. The weather's beautiful!" It was one of the rare times when we were traveling that I felt safe; one those infrequent times when I let my guard down. What could possibly go wrong? It was a perfect November day, or so I thought.

We started out early in the morning; there was literally no traffic on the roads. And then on the road was a little frost—then a curve, a semi, and as my husband looked in the rear view mirror he saw our sons' car slide out of control in front of the semi. Our sons were killed in an instant. No survival kit would have helped. The morning, which had been so bright, beautiful, and blue became pitch–black. "Out of the blue" our sons were killed. "Out of the blue" the sky came falling down on that fateful day. Their deaths caught us totally off guard and off balance. Nothing could have been more unexpected.

About a month after the accident a bereaved parent couple visited us and shared how they had seemed to receive visits, calls, or letters from "angels," both known and unknown, whenever they were at a particularly low point in their grief. They were confident that the angels would be there for us as well—to lift us out of the deep valleys when we questioned how we could possibly keep on going on. We were also told that there would be no predicting who our angels might be—some would even be strangers—but in any event, the angels would be there when we needed them. They would appear "out of the blue," out of nowhere. And so it was, and so it has continued to be.

Over the years, the "out of the blue" angels have shown their true "color" by continuing to take the time and make the effort to provide support. Several of my sons' friends honored them by asking if they could have one of their personal items as a memento. Each request was prefaced by the story about how that personal item was connected with their friendship. Even though sorting through Erik's and David's possessions was gut-wrenching beyond belief, there was meaning in knowing who would appreciate having my son's guitar, tennis racquet, Monet print, mirror, or golf club. By and large these mementos did not have any significant monetary value, but the emotional value was incalculable.

Similarly, several friends found meaning in giving us gifts that were representative of their relationship with our sons. These items would typically reflect something humorous, serious, or quirky about Erik or David—those passions, idiosyncrasies, or beliefs that made the friends' relationships with our sons special. These "out of the blue" gifts, such as a painting, poem, song, picture, or ceramic piece, became concrete connections with our sons that no price tag could begin to match.

As time went on, we received other tributes that let us know how our sons continued to influence the lives of their friends. About six months after the accident, a short note of reflections brought comfort to my heart. Knowing David well, having worked with him at summer tennis camps, this friend shared his admiration for David's teaching ability and unusually high energy level, but at the same time was honest enough to admit that these feelings had also been tinged with jealousy and the need to compete with him. This friend told how he was continuing that competitive spirit every day by rating his coaching performance against an imaginary "Dave Level" scale. Almost three years after the initial correspondence, another shorter note, two sentences long, came "out of the blue" from this same friend. He related that he believed that David had played an important role in the success he had with his tennis team that year, attributing much of his championship season to consistently being able to give himself a 6–8 score on his "Dave Level" scale. He concluded by saying he thought we "might want to know."

This friend could not begin to imagine what it meant to this bereaved mom to receive the follow-up note confirming that the thoughts expressed in the original correspondence continued to hold true. Knowing that David continued to be a very strong motivating force in keeping this friend "pumped up" each and every day was an incredibly powerful tribute. This went well beyond remembering. The comment that we "might want to know" was an understatement; we needed to know.

As is obvious from this story, reflections or tributes do not need to be lengthy to be meaningful. Mere sentences can speak volumes. No recollection or remembrance is too insignificant to share. To the contrary, regardless of how long it has been since the loss, sharing these thoughts with the bereaved would likely be a source of comfort and meaning.

Other bereaved parents have mentioned how surprised and touched they have been by "out of the blue" tributes, public or private, that were made with the express intent of including their children in a special event. Friends or family members, especially those who live in a small town, could place a public tribute in the form of an ad or editorial in the local newspaper. A loved one could also be remembered at celebrations such as weddings, baptisms, or family reunions, with flowers or candles, along with a short note in the program or bulletin, describing the relationship. At class reunions, concerts, or camps, time could be set aside for sharing stories or memories. Erik's classmates let us know he had been symbolically included in his ten-year high school reunion by giving us a beautiful handmade card and generous memorial. Wanting to include David in the wedding party of one of his best friends, the best man wore a symbolic T-shirt under his tuxedo shirt. There was a strong feeling that David's spirit was sharing the event with them.

The "out of the blue" tribute that blew me away came from someone who did not even know my sons. On the first anniversary of their deaths, two candles were placed close together on one of the protruding bricks on the wall behind the church altar. It was powerful. Without knowing it, this person had chosen a symbol that had a meaningful connection to my sons. For several Christmas seasons Erik and David had climbed that same wall to place votive candles on the protruding bricks, and to make the task more interesting, they had challenged each other to see who could get his candle to the highest point. Subsequently, during the next two Christmas seasons there were two candles placed close together on the highest protruding brick on the wall. There was, appropriately, no explanation in the bulletin; some may have known, others may have wondered, and still others may not have noticed at all. But I knew and appreciated that in a silent but very moving way, my sons had been included in the service.

At different times other angels checked in to let us know that our sons were remembered. While calls, visits, cards, or flowers arrived on significant occasions, such as their birthdays, holidays, or their death date, the surprise was who remembered. One of David's friends, who had not communicated with him for years prior to his death, sent flowers "out of the blue" two years after the accident. Another friend left this message on the answering machine: "Thinking of you— it's Mother's Day" thoughtfully omitting the "happy" part of the greeting. And then there were those "out of the blue" occasions that have no connection with a day at all. My husband received a call from a person with whom he had no regular contact, stating, "I really don't know why I'm calling you, except I was thinking of my children [who were alive] and then I thought of your children, and I just had to call."

Additional years passed. As Mother's Day, 2000, approached, my heart was weighed down with deep sadness. I found myself thinking, "I need one person, just one person, to recognize how the death of my sons has changed my perception of this day."

At the time of these reflections I was scheduled for a follow-up visit after some minor surgery. The surgeon had heard about my sons' deaths and acknowledged my loss on the day of surgery. One of his first questions on this return visit was to ask me, "Is your [surviving] son coming home for Mother's Day?" I responded by saying the distance factor precluded their coming. He then continued, *"This has got to be a difficult weekend for you.* I'll be thinking of you." His voice and demeanor were genuine and sincere; this was no obligatory comment— he meant it. He then asked some questions that indicated that he knew some specific details about the tragedy. The gift of those questions invited me to talk for a few minutes about the accident and how it had changed the way I lived my life. Again he said that he would be thinking of me on Mother's Day. As he walked out of the room, he had sprouted the wings of an angel.

"Out of the blue" my request had been granted. One person, basically a stranger, had acknowledged my sadness. My heart had been warmed and I felt comforted. But the story doesn't end there. On Mother's Day the doorbell rang. Holding a vase with the most beautiful bouquet of pink tulips I had ever seen was the surgeon and his family, who said, "We're thinking of you." In my imagination, Erik and David were standing there with them.

These "out of the blue" remembrances were truly from unexpected angels. They came at times when I needed to have my ongoing grief acknowledged and to be reassured that my sons were remembered. After experiencing one of these kind and sensitive gestures, I have frequently thought, "What an angel!" And yet, I would guess that these people would be surprised or even amused, that their "out of the blue" kind and thoughtful actions had been perceived as angelic. But, perhaps, that is a characteristic of earthly angels: they are completely unaware of the significant impact their caring gestures have on grievers. Another attribute of these angels appeared to be the uncanny timing of their appearance. Did they really sense when support was needed, or could it be that any time would be a good time to provide support to those who were mourning?

It would be impossible for anyone to go through life without darkness at some point turning one's day into night. With some losses the day becomes gray, with others it becomes dark, and with a catastrophic loss the day becomes pitch-black. When angels come "out of the blue" to provide support and love, they bring light into the pain-filled darkness. Any light that penetrates the darkness will be treasured for all time.

REFLECTIONS ABOUT ANGELS

Friends are angels
who lift us up
when our wings
forget how to fly.

RUTH JOY, INC.
GREAT FALLS, MT

We are, each of us,
an angel
with only one wing.
and we can fly only
by embracing each other.

A BEREAVED PARENT

GIFTS FROM THE HEART:
TREASURES FOREVER

My perception of gift giving changed significantly following the deaths of Erik and David. I have always been uncomfortable when the monetary value of a gift becomes the standard that signifies whether one is or is not loved. Equally disconcerting are those gifts that are given with the expectation that the debit/credit sheet for the gift-giving component of the relationship will eventually be balanced out with a reciprocal gift of comparable monetary value. Then there are those gifts for which the only motivation is to express appreciation and love. These gifts may be a letter, card, e-mail, or some item that symbolizes what is valued about the relationship. The monetary value, if there is any, is not important; the real treasure is that these gifts come from the heart.

Gifts from the Heart, Received: The most valuable gift that any person could receive, anytime, anywhere, and anyplace, is unconditional love. Much has been written and said about unconditional love— feeling loved for one's inherent value as a person, while at the same time understanding and accepting that what one does may not always be perceived as being lovable.

When I have been given the freedom to grieve and encouraged to plot my own map for my grief journey, I have felt loved for who I am regardless of how well I was or was not grieving. Communicating unconditional love is certainly easier said than done, but when I have experienced it, I was aware that I had received a gift from the heart or, as some might say, undeserved grace.

Other gifts from the heart have spoken to the essence of friendship. Three years post-loss my husband and I were honored to receive two gifts, one for each of our sons. The first of these gifts was from one of David's college friends. David's favorite author was Robert Fulghum, of *All I Ever Really Needed to Know, I learned in Kindergarten* fame. This friend saw Fulghum's newest book, *Words I Wish I Wrote,* in a bookstore and remembered the times she and David had read his words of wisdom to each other. Knowing that David would have liked the book, she purchased one for us. Along with the book came a note of how David's values about life and people had influenced her approach to life, and how knowing this had helped keep his spirit alive within her heart.

A few days later we received an anonymous letter from one of Erik's high school friends on what would have been his thirtieth birthday. This friend related some memories of Erik's personal qualities and characteristics and how, with additional years of life experiences this friend had recognized the breadth and depth of Erik's values. This anonymous angel expressed gratitude for having been lucky enough to have known our son and let us know how Erik continued to influence this friend's life.

Both of these letters were truly gifts from the heart, from the spirit—spontaneous, unexpected, and reflective. More important, these individuals recognized that their relationship with my sons had far greater lasting value on their lives than things having monetary significance.

Gifts from the Heart, Given: Despite all the doubts and questions I have, there has been one thing I have known with absolute certainty. I know that my sons knew they were loved, appreciated, and respected. How do I know that? Because they both received letters prior to their deaths that told them so—told Erik what a good physical therapist he was going to be; told David how, as a teacher and coach, he was making a difference in the lives of so many kids. People had not only told them these things, *they had written them down.* Erik and David knew!

I also knew because of the many times my husband or I were approached in a store, at work, in church, or via telephone calls and told about one of Erik and David's kind deeds, how much they cared about people, how they used humor to illustrate a point, or just what great kids they were. We always passed the kind words on to them. No one can ever be told too much that they are loved, appreciated and respected. They knew!

After the tragedy the entire faculty and staff of David's school, his colleagues and friends, received a letter from the school's superintendent. In that letter he reflected on the fragility of life and emphasized the importance of expressing our love, respect, and appreciation of each other more often. Then he gave everyone some homework. The assignment was to sit down and write a note to at least three staff members telling them they were appreciated and what made them special.

To illustrate the potential outcome of such an assignment, and how the power of a message can transcend time, consider this story that took place years ago. A teacher of a third-grade class was concerned about all the bickering and fighting that was occurring on the playground. So she gave each student the assignment of writing one characteristic that they liked about each of their classmates. Each student then received a copy of all the positive statements that had been written about them. A number of years later one of these students, then a young man, was killed in Vietnam. In his billfold they found the paper stating what his classmates had said they liked about him years ago. It had obviously been folded and unfolded many times.

After hearing this story at the young man's funeral, several classmates pulled out their billfolds and purses and showed that they, too, had been carrying around their papers for all those years. Billfolds do not carry junk; they carry information that is important to have readily available such as credit cards, proof of insurance, cash, driver's license, *and treasures*—pictures of loved ones, poems, or even words written years ago—that affirm one's worth as a human being. Words that said they were loved, appreciated, or respected—gifts from the heart, treasures forever.

Taking the time and making the effort to recognize another's accomplishments or acts of kindness is one of those gifts that will be remembered over time. A key prerequisite must be that any words spoken or written are 100 percent genuine. In other words, whatever is said or written must be expressed with absolute conviction, no hedging. An insincere compliment does not ring true. If a performance cannot be sincerely praised, then perhaps their attitude and/or effort, excellent sportsmanship, or markedly improved execution of a skill could be complimented. Focus on what is really done well. The old adage about catching someone doing something right and then recognizing it has much merit.

Another reality is that the fragility of life should not be underestimated. Paraphrasing Emerson a bit: You cannot give a gift from the heart too soon, for you never know how soon it will be too late. There are no guarantees or promises that there will be another today or tomorrow; life can change in a moment.

Erik's closest friend wrote him a letter after his death sharing what he had meant to her. In the last lines of her letter were these words. "I never told you that you meant so much to me…I hope you know now that I love you." She had taken for granted that they would be friends for a lifetime. It was not to be. She took this lesson in life to heart and wasted no time in writing or calling her other friends to tell them how much she valued her friendships with them.

So while there's still time, it's important to seize the moment and write, e-mail, fax, or tell those important to you how knowing them has been one of life's treasures. Even if they already know, something written would make it "official." Words written have a way of confirming words spoken. And a meaningful letter or note can be kept in a safe place, such as a billfold, where it can be pulled out and reread over time.

Gifts from the heart are gifts treasured. I will be forever thankful that my sons received these gifts of the heart prior to their deaths, affirming that they were loved, they were respected, and they were appreciated. They knew! I know!

And as I continue to receive these gifts from the heart, I know my sons are still loved, are still appreciated, and are still respected. I can only hope they know!

Now it has become my responsibility to give gifts from the heart to those I love, to those I appreciate, and to those I respect—so they know.

A single real friend is a treasure
worth more than gold or precious stones.

Money can buy many things,
good or evil.

All the wealth of the world
could not buy a friend or pay you
for the loss of one.

ANONYMOUS

What matters to me in life is not where I live
or when I die but rather how I live
and with whom I share my life,
my experiences, and my love...

As long as I am loved
and as long as there is someone to hold my hand,
it does not matter to me when or how I die.

ERIK AASEN
FALL 1993
GERONTOLOGY PAPER

A LEGACY OF LIVING:
WALK IN THE WORLD
FOR US

About two months after the accident, there was a front page story in the local paper titled "A Story of Living: Remembering the Legacy of Erik and David Aasen."

The article described Erik's and David's commitment to excellence, their strong ethics and values, their selfless compassion, their ability to take a problem and turn it into a challenge or opportunity, their wholesome use of humor, and their exemplary sportsmanship. They were able to motivate others to believe in themselves and their potential because they believed in the inherent goodness and worth of each person. They genuinely respected everyone, which was reciprocated by people of all ages. The article summarized their legacy with the words, "They taught those who knew them how to live."

While Erik and David shared many values and goals, each took his own unique road to achieve them. Erik was a reflective thinker who had a passion for learning; he believed that there was something to be learned from literally every situation. Following a period of soul-searching for a meaningful vocation, Erik decided to combine his love for physical conditioning, the sciences, and service to others into a career as a physical therapist. He usually stayed in the background, quietly motivating, supporting or mentoring others experiencing difficulties. Erik had the courage of his convictions and never hesitated to advocate for those who were oppressed and exploited. He was not openly affectionate, but his compassion and sensitivity to others were extraordinary. The extrovert part of Erik would surface when he would surprise his classmates with an impression, for example, of Paul Harvey in Spanish, which resulted in hysterical laughter. Erik loved playing volleyball, was fascinated with dinosaurs, and was an ardent Star Trek fan.

David's personality tended to thrust him into the spotlight. He was a spontaneous hugger whose smile would light up a room. Besides having an imagination and quick wit that knew no bounds, David's level of enthusiasm and energy were hard to match. He loved to play practical jokes, but laughed hardest when the joke was on himself. David was a modern-day Pied Piper with students; they loved being with him not only for what he taught them about math and tennis but what he taught them about life. He expected his students to give their best effort, and they usually rose to the challenge. He was born to be a teacher. When he looked at the stars on a moonlit night or held his newborn nephew in his arms, he was awed by the wonders and marvels of creation. When his friends or students were hurting, so was he.

As a gift to his "Friends Forever," David's signature quote, "The grass is green, the sky is blue, it's a great day to be alive" was framed and given to a countless number of friends and students.

I wanted to give a similar gift to Erik's friends; since he did not have a signature quote, I wrote "Walk in The World for Us." This piece reflects both Erik's and David's values, what they stood for, and what they believed in. It, too, is their legacy of living.

WALK IN THE WORLD FOR US.
Make God's world a better place.

Care for the earth, its land, water, air,
so the sun will light the day and the
moon and stars the night, the water will
be clear, the grass green, the sky blue.

Witness to the need for justice, peace, and
equality by building bridges to cooperation
and being a voice for the oppressed and
exploited.

Treat all you meet with respect, honesty,
and dignity, so each person feels
empowered to reach his or her potential.

Minister to those experiencing loss through
the lifelines of your presence, your
actions and words of support, and your prayers.

Share your gifts of time, talents, and money
with others, along with a good dose of humor
and fun, so the blessings you've been given can
be multiplied.

Nurture your valued relationships with family
and friends; share with them an ever-ready
dazzling smile, give many hugs, and much love.

In everything you do, be the best you can
be; work hard, learn hard, play hard!
Live life to the fullest!

WALK IN THE WORLD FOR US.
Make God's world a better place
so that every day will be a
great day to be alive!!

APRIL, 1995

187

Postscript: In ending "Walk In The World For Us" with a part of David's signature quote, "It's a great day to be alive," I was well aware that it was highly unlikely that either of them had experienced an extremely high-intensity loss in their abbreviated lives. In contrast, for those experiencing the aftermath of a catastrophic loss, proclaiming that "It's a great day to be alive" and truly meaning it might be a bit of a stretch. Rather, with the energies and efforts of many bereaved focused on finding a purpose or mission in life, it would likely be more honest to rephrase the last lines to read,

WALK IN THE WORLD FOR US.
Make God's world a better place
so that every day there will be
meaning in being alive.

"Human beings do not live forever.
We live less than the time it takes to blink an eye,
if we measure our lives against eternity."

"So it may be asked what value is there to a human life
when there is so much pain in the world?
What does it mean to have to suffer so much if our lives
are nothing more than the blink of an eye?"

He paused again, his eyes misty now, then went on.
"I learned a long time ago,
that a blink of an eye in itself is nothing.
But the eye that blinks, that is something."

"A span of life is nothing.
But the man who lives that span, he is something.
He can fill that tiny span with meaning,
so its quality is immeasurable
though its quantity may be insignificant."

CHAIM POTOK

CHOOSING A MONUMENT:
A LASTING PUBLIC TRIBUTE

One of the details that went with the decision of having an earth burial was determining what kind of monument should be placed at their graves. When selecting Erik's and David's memorials a few months after their deaths, I had two goals. First, it was important that their graves be marked with their names as soon as possible. Then, since I was still trying to wrap my head around the totally incomprehensible fact that these markers were for MY SONS, the other driving force was to bite the bullet and get it over with. So while we were still in a profound state of shock, my husband and I purchased two small slightly, slanted stones that listed their names, birth and death dates, and a short phrase about each of them.

As time went on, I began regarding their markers with a sense of uneasiness because they did little to define Erik's and David's personalities and philosophy of life. In being one of the more lasting public tributes, these monuments fell far short of reflecting, in a meaningful way, who they were and what they stood for. Moreover, living in a climate where snow blanketed the ground periodically for up to five months, their markers were frequently covered with snow. Since it was unacceptable to have their names covered up, with each snowfall I made it a point to go out and clear the snow away.

One of the many lessons Erik's and David's deaths taught me centered on the fragility of life. Not knowing how much time may be left, my husband and I decided that if their memorials were going to be changed, it was important that it become a priority sooner rather than later. Sooner, in this situation, was more than seven years after my sons' deaths. While that certainly stretched the definition of sooner, once the decision was made, a monument company was contacted and the design process began in earnest.

Their new monuments mark their place in this world. Besides their names and life dates on the front, the star-and-crescent-moon symbol provides a meaningful link to the "Walk in the World for Us, Make God's World a Better Place" sentence. A solar-powered Peace Light, illuminating the darkness each evening, symbolizes how the light that their lives radiated on others has continued to shine. And with the upright monuments it would take a lot of snow to cover up their names.

David's picture and the symbols for his life clearly proclaim that he was "Born to Be a Teacher" and a tennis enthusiast. Those who knew David recognize TLC as the acronym for Tennis and Life Camps (Gustavus Adolphus College, St. Peter, MN), where he had been an instructor/supervisor for several summers. As the universally accepted acronym for tender loving care, TLC is what everyone needs for their well-being.

Erik's commitment to a healthy lifestyle and love of learning is reflected in the graphic on his stone. His picture captures how "his intense love for life lives on." This same inscription is on a plaque by a tree dedicated in honor of his memory at his alma mater, Hope College, in Holland, MI. The other obvious symbol of the word *HOPE* is the human need to have hope as an integral part of one's life at all times but especially following a tragedy.

Together the acronym *TLC* and the word *HOPE* symbolize what Erik and David believed would help make the world a better place.

And as for the original headstones? They were reset as foot markers. Coming to the point where we were comfortable with how our sons' legacy was represented on their monuments provided some solace as my husband and I continued on with our grief journey.

PROLOGUE

Cut off in mid–sentence, your life remains
A mere prologue, thus...
A book of blank pages where
There should have been adventures.

I pick up your life's open volume
And wonder what might have been written.
Would your story have been straight and true
Or bent before the challenges you faced?
Would the promises of your prologue have been fulfilled
Or disappointment been your course?

Never to know the progress of your tale
I am suspended in doubt.
Must you remain forever a prologue
Or could I write a script
And through my life state your meaning?

Yes, I will present your messages.
Love, compassion, commitment, and knowledge.
These truths will speak through my pages
Making your prologue—forever mine.

ADAPTED FROM MARCIA ALIG
COMPASSIONATE FRIENDS CHAPTER
MERCER AREA (NEW JERSEY)
JUNE, 1981

A CHILD'S LEGACY

What would be the legacy of a child who has died too soon? Many bereaved parents ask themselves with a sense of fear, "How will my child be remembered?" A primary factor contributing to my fear was the fact that Erik and David did not have a chance to leave their indelible "mark" in the world by having children — the mechanism by which stories about the family history are typically passed down to future generations. And, with fewer numbers in the next generation to carry on the family traditions and stories, there was perhaps an additional fear that I would be forgotten as well.

There are certainly other ways to be remembered: perhaps through choosing a profession that focuses on service to others, maybe by volunteering in the community, possibly by being a whiz at something, or maybe by being an advocate for some worthwhile cause. There are countless ways of leaving a meaningful legacy. But when a child has died, it seems that they did not have enough time to leave a legacy. How, then, can one's child be remembered?

When a young adult dies, there is likely a strong indication of all that he or she would have done to make a positive difference in the lives of others. I had the blessing of knowing that my sons were making great strides in doing their part to make this world a better place through their chosen vocations and with values and attributes that gave them a rock-solid foundation for caring about and reaching out to others. But knowing that has also contributed mightily to my grief.

When a child dies in the years of childhood or adolescence, there are inklings, just a tease, of what would have been. The pain that comes from not knowing more about who he or she would have become, of never being able to know more, is also agonizing in its intensity.

For those whose children died prior to their birth, shortly after birth, or as babes, never to sleep in anything but a crib, there is a loss of the promise and hope of being surprised at what they would have become. Besides having a limited bank of memories and pictures, not knowing anything about their potential, or dreams, or what their good works might have accomplished may add to the devastation of their death.

The death of a child, any child, also has a lifelong impact on the community in which he or she would have lived. When a child dies, at any age, that community has lost part of its future. Lost for all time is what those children could have contributed to make a difference in their corners of the world if their lives had been lived out to their fullest measure.

But there is one thing that death cannot take away and that is the name of any child who has died before his or her time. The first gift parents give their newly born son or daughter is a name. In making that choice, different options for the first and middle names may be written out to see how they looked with the last name. Or perhaps these names were spoken out loud, in order to hear which combination sounded the best. Perhaps it was important that a child's name had a family connection. Much love, thought, and time is usually spent in choosing a name that give one's son or daughter a space and place in the world that is just for them, including an identity that followed them all through their lives and, now, after their deaths.

This means that whenever their names are linked with a meaningful memory, whenever they have made a difference in the life of another, whenever an act of kindness is done in their name, these children have been remembered. Their names, in being symbolic of who they were, become their primary legacy.

WE'RE SO ALIKE, YOU AND I

We're so alike, you and I
I lost a daughter.
You lost a son.
She was eight months old.
He was thirty-seven.
She never spoke.
He called you every Sunday.
She died nine years ago.
He's been buried two months now.
I always look at babies.
You see all the young fathers.
I miss my daughter.
You miss your son.
You see,
We're so alike,
You and I.

CATHY HEIDER
THE COMPASSIONATE FRIENDS
ALGONA, IA

THE COMPASSIONATE FRIENDS WORLDWIDE CANDLE LIGHTING

A common theme among many bereaved parents is their wish to have their children remembered. Born out of an idea that was made possible by the Internet, The Compassionate Friends *Worldwide Candle Lighting* does just that. This event, which began in 1997, has grown dramatically every year, confirming the importance of having a day set aside to remember all children who have died. With the multiple emotions and cultural pressures associated with the holiday season, it was appropriate that The Compassionate Friends chose the second Sunday in December for this memorial event.

This meaningful time of remembrance is held for one hour in each local time zone beginning at 7:00 p.m. Just like the handoff of a baton in a relay race, the candle lighting starts at the International Date line and moves west through each time zone. As the candles burn down in one time zone, they are lighted in the next, illuminating the globe in a virtual twenty-four hour wave of light. Hundreds of formal memorial services held by chapters of The Compassionate Friends and other organizations have joined in this remembrance. At the same time, thousands more candles are lighted quietly in homes or parks where family and friends gather to share memories, watch videos, or view pictures.

As a multitude of bereaved families join together to light candles for our sons and daughters, brothers and sisters, grandsons and granddaughters throughout the world, there is a tangible feeling that we are not alone in our grief. Seeing the brilliance of these "lights of love" honoring all children who have died before their time is powerful. Having a shared time to publicly express our ongoing love for them as a local, national, and global community is meaningful. As these candles beam their light throughout the world, the message is crystal clear—the light of our children will always shine on with love in our hearts and in our lives.

In 1999, the *Worldwide Candle Lighting* became a regional event encompassing a forty-mile radius around Mankato, Minnesota; candles were lighted in a countless number of homes, church bells rang in tandem with the candle lighting, and bereaved parents were given the gift of seeing their children's names grace the pages of their local newspapers. How did that happen? Publicity made the difference.

Having learned about the memorial event through reading the national magazine of The Compassionate Friends, *We Need Not Walk Alone*, I shared this information with our local hospice staff and that was all it took. With hospice sponsoring the commemoration, bereaved parents learned through church bulletins, newspapers, and other media that with a signed consent their child's name, birth date, and death date would be published in the regional paper. The response exceeded all expectations. With just over a week to respond, parents bombarded the paper with the names of more than a hundred children who had died too soon. More than thirty names missed the deadline, and other parents called after seeing the paper to ask how their child's name could be included in the remembrance the next year. Death dates ranged from 1949 to 1999, and children's ages ranged from newborns to young adults.

The stories told following the candle lighting affirmed the importance of this event. There were stories of parents who saw their child's name in print or heard their names spoken for the first time in years. Parents were finally given permission to break years of silence and speak about their deeply missed child. One bereaved parent shared how she was the last one alive to remember her child and hoped that one day there would be a permanent listing of names in a public place where her daughter's name could be forever engraved in stone. (That wish has been fulfilled with the construction of a children's memorial that was spearheaded by a locally based bereaved parents group, One Bright Star. Located in a city park, this memorial now includes her child's name and that of many others imprinted on a paver or plaque.) Other stories told of how this day of remembrance affirmed and validated the gift of their sons' or daughters' lives, however short their time.

An additional benefit of this worldwide commemoration is that friends and family members are also given an opportunity to bring up a deceased child's name in conversation. When a child has died, family and friends may have intended to share their memories with the bereaved family at "the right time," but often "the time had never seemed right." Now the *Worldwide Candle Lighting* has provided a time—a second chance—for them to act on their intentions of weeks, months, or years past and share their reflections, stories, and memories.

Every year more bereaved families are learning about this wonderful memorial opportunity. The *Worldwide Candle Lighting* has been publicized in the media through Parade magazine, Ann Landers' column (and Annie's Mailbox), *Guidepost* magazine, and hundreds of newspapers as well as dozens of television and radio stations across the country. The Compassionate Friends is increasing its publicity each year and encouraging allied organizations to participate. Those posting memorial messages on that day at The Compassionate Friends Web site (**www.compassionatefriends.org**) now number in the thousands. This event holds great promise in helping the world's families to bring their grief out of the closet and into an open, nonjudgmental atmosphere.

At the rising of the sun and its going down
We remember them,

In the blowing of the wind and in the chill of winter
We remember them,

In the opening of the buds and in the rebirth of spring
We remember them,

In the rustling of the leaves and in the beauty of autumn
We remember them,

In the beginning of the year and when it ends
We remember them,

When we are weary and in need of strength
We remember them,

When we are lost and sick at heart,
We remember them,

When we have moments of meaning we yearn to share,
We remember them,

So long as we live they too shall live for

They are now a part of us as

We remember them.

GATES OF PRAYER
JEWISH PRAYER BOOK, 1975

BIBLIOGRAPHY

Boehler, Tony. "A Story of Living: Remembering the Legacy of Erik and David Aasen." *St. Peter Herald,* 9 February 1995, p. 1.

Finkbeiner, Ann K. *After the Death of a Child: Living with Loss through the Years.* New York: The Free Press, 1996.

Fulghum, Robert. *Words I Wish I Wrote.* New York: HarperCollins Publishers, 1997.

Goodman, Ellen. "Let's Add Closure to All of This Talk about Healing." *Boston Globe,* 4 January 1998, p. 7.

Heavilin, Marilyn, and Matthew Heavilin. *Grief Is a Family Affair.* Menifee, C A: The Proverbial Solution, 2000.

Kagan (Klein), Henya. *Gili's Book: A Journey into Bereavement for Parents and Counselors.* New York: Teachers College Press, 1998.

Kagan (Klein), Henya. "On Signs and Signals." *We Need Not Walk Alone* (spring 2001).

Klass, Dennis. "Bereaved Parents' Continuing Bond with Their Children." *Death Studies 17,* no. 4 (1993): 343-368.

Knapp, Ronald. *Beyond Endurance: After the Death of a Child.* New York: Schocken Books, 1986.

Kushner, Harold S. *When Bad Things Happen to Good People.* New York: Avon Books, 1981.

Lewis, C.S. *A Grief Observed.* New York: Seabury Press, 1961.

Morrell, David. *Fireflies.* New York: Warner Books, 1988.

Riches, Gordon, and Pam Dawson. (1996). "Community of Feeling: The Culture of Bereaved Parents." *Mortality* 1, no. 2 (1996): 163–161.

Rosof, Barbara. *The Worst Loss: How Families Heal from the Death of a Child.* New York: Henry Holt, 1994.

Schneider, John M. *Finding My Way.* Colfax, WI: Seasons Press, 1994.

Sittser, Gerald L. *A Grace Disguised.* Grand Rapids, MI: Zondervan Publishing House, 1996.

Wolterstorff, Nicholas. *Lament for a Son.* Grand Rapids, MI: William B. Erdmans Publishing Company, 1987.

Woods, Kay. *Visions of the Bereaved.* Pittsburgh, PA: Sterling House, 1998.

IF ONLY, ONE MORE TIME...

To hear your voice loud and clear,
To see your image as if you're here,
To feel your warmth like you are near,
If only, one more time...

To hear you call, "Mom, I'm home,"
To keep me company when I'm alone,
To watch you run and grab the phone,
If only, one more time...

To watch you sit quietly and read,
To buy you things you say you need,
To see you do a thoughtful deed,
If only, one more time...

To find a note written by you,
To walk upstairs and trip over your shoe,
To comfort you when you're feeling blue,
If only, one more time...

To feel your arms in a firm embrace,
To see the smile upon your face,
To understand when you needed space,
If only, one more time.

IF ONLY, ONE MORE TIME...

COMPASSIONATE FRIENDS NEWSLETTER
Fairmont Chapter
Fairmont, MN

GRIEF RESOURCES

Support Group Organizations

The Compassionate Friends, Inc.
(Bereaved parents and their families)
P.O. Box 3696
Oak Brook, IL 60522
1-877-969-0010
www.compassionatefriends.com

National SIDS Infant Death Program Support Center
(Sudden Infant Death Syndrome)
1314 Bedford Ave., Suite 210
Baltimore, MD 21208
1-800-638-7437
www.sids-id-psc.org

American Foundation for Suicide Prevention
(Survivors of Suicide)
120 Wall St., 22nd Floor
New York, NY 10005
1-888-333-AFSP
www.afsp.org

National SHARE Office
(SHARE Pregnancy and Infant Loss Support, Inc.)
St. Joseph Health Center
300 First Capitol Drive
St. Charles, MO 63301
1-800-829-6819
www.nationalshareoffice.com

Alive Alone
(loss of an only child or all children)
11115 Dull Robinson Road
VanWert, OH 45891
www.alivealone.org

National Parents of Murdered Children
(POMC)
100 East Eighth St. Suite B-41
Cincinnati, OH 45202
1-888-818-POMC
www.pomc.com

GRIEF RESOURCES (CONTINUED)

Support Groups in Print

We Need Not Walk Alone
(four issues/yr)
The Compassionate Friends, Inc.
P.O. Box 3696
Oak Brook, Il 60522
1-877-969-0010
www.compassionatefriends.com

Bereavement Magazine
(six issues/yr)
4765 North Carefree Circle
Colorado Springs, CO 80917
1-888-604-4673
www.breavementmag.com

Parents of Murdered Children
(three issues/yr)
100 E, 8th St. B-41
Cincinnati, OH 45202

A Grief Catalog of Grief Resources

Centering Corporation, Inc.
P.O. Box 4600
Omaha, NE 68104
402-553-1200
www.centering.org

In-Sight Books, Inc.
P.O. Box 42467
Oklahoma City, OK 73123
1-800-658-9262
www.insightbooks.com

ABOUT THE AUTHOR

Nita Aasen earned her undergraduate nursing degree from the University Of Minnesota School of Nursing and a master's degree in Health Science from Minnesota State University, Mankato. She has worked in hospitals in both rural and urban settings, as a nursing instructor and, for the last sixteen years, in public health. Working in the obstetrical unit, medical surgical areas and the emergency room brought a myriad of contacts with those confronting death and dying, loss and grief. As a nursing instructor at a small private liberal arts college, she brought these educational and clinical experiences to the classroom. Years later, when her two young adult sons, Erik and David, were killed she learned how little she truly knew about grief.

Many of Nita's essays have been published in two national grief support magazines: *We Need Not Walk Alone,* a publication of Compassionate Friends, Inc., and *Bereavement* magazine. Nita's column, "Giving Voice to the Grief Experience" became a regular feature of *Bereavement* magazine beginning with the November/December, 2003 issue.

NOW I KNOW

I never knew, when you lost your child,
What you were going through.
I wasn't there, I stayed away.
I just deserted you.
I didn't know the words to say,
I didn't know the things to do.
I think your pain so frightened me,
I didn't know how to comfort you.
And then one day my child died.
You were the first one there.
You quietly stayed by my side, listened,
And held me as I cried.
You didn't leave, you didn't go.
The lesson learned is—NOW I KNOW.

ALICE KERR, TCF, LOWER BUCKS, PA

LIVING STILL, LOVING ALWAYS
ESSAYS OF A BEREAVED PARENT

Copies of this book can be ordered through our website:
www.wilsonpublishinghouse.com
or
Mail this form with check or money order to:
Wilson Publishing House
720 N. 3rd Street
St. Peter, MN 56082

ORDER FORM

NAME_____

ADDRESS_____

CITY_____

STATE_____ ZIP _____

EMAIL_____

PAYMENT   (circle one)   CHECK   MONEY ORDER

ORDER QTY _____ x $10.95 (MN residents add 6.5%) $_____

Shipping* $_____

TOTAL $_____

*$3.00 shipping first item, $1.50 each additional item.
Mail to: Wilson Publishing House
                720 N. 3rd Street, St. Peter, MN 56082

WILSON
PUBLISHING
HOUSE